T5-AFT-397

JUST SAY, "YES"!

TODAY IS THE DAY TO—

- GET RID OF NEGATIVE FEELINGS

- FIND THE POWER WITHIN YOU

- GET OUT OF YOUR COCOON

- FEEL GOOD ABOUT YOURSELF

- THINK, SPEAK, AND ACT WITH CONFIDENCE

- OPEN UP TO RELATIONSHIPS

- MOVE AHEAD ON THE JOB

- STAY HEALTHY

- LOOK YOUR BEST

- BE PROUD OF BECOMING THE PERSON YOU WANT TO BE

EMPOWER YOURSELF

Every Woman's Guide to Self-Esteem

ADA P. KAHN, M.P.H. and SHEILA KIMMEL, M.A.

AVON BOOKS ◆ NEW YORK

''She Gave Herself a Rose'' by Kristin Lems. Copyright © 1994 by Kleine Ding Music, Inc. (BMI). Used by permission.

''We Are All Flowers'' adapted from *Touching Peace: Practicing the Art of Mindful Living* by Thich Nhat Hanh, Parallax Press, Berkeley, California, 1992. Reprinted by permission.

AVON BOOKS
A division of
The Hearst Corporation
1350 Avenue of the Americas
New York, New York 10019

Copyright © 1997 by Ada P. Kahn and Sheila Kimmel
Published by arrangement with the authors
Library of Congress Catalog Card Number: 96-96428
ISBN: 0-380-77094-6

First Avon Books Printing: January 1997

AVON TRADEMARK REG. U.S. PAT. OFF. AND IN OTHER COUNTRIES, MARCA REGISTRADA, HECHO EN U.S.A.

Printed in the U.S.A.

RA   10 9 8 7 6 5 4 3 2 1

ACKNOWLEDGMENTS

We want to thank our daughters, Ruth Kahn Wells and Laurie Kimmel, for their love, encouragement, and suggestions while we were writing this book. Sheila particularly thanks her husband, Fred Kimmel, for his devotion and support. We appreciate our many friends who shared life stories with us (names in most cases have been changed).

We thank Dorothy Young Riess, M.D., Pasadena, California, for her suggestions for overcoming perfection and Pamela A. Mohr, Center on Children and the Law, American Bar Association, Washington, D.C., for her comments on education for women and sexual harassment. We thank Dale S. Gody, Ph.D., a psychotherapist in Wilmette, Illinois, for suggestions on communication skills for couples after the arrival of a baby.

We thank Roxanne Barton Conlin, Des Moines, for sharing her life story; Linda Carli, Ph.D., Wellesley College, for details on the importance of competency as well as warmth in the workplace; and Linda Holt, M.D., Evanston, Illinois, for her comments on working mothers.

We appreciate the comments on career planning from Joyce Simon, past president, American Women's Society of Certified Public Accountants and comments on harassment from Carol Kleiman, *Chicago Tribune*.

We are grateful to Ada P. Kahn and Jan Fawcett, M.D., co-authors, *The Encyclopedia of Mental Health* (Facts on File, Inc., 1993), for sharing material on choosing mental health professionals.

We thank Parallax Press, Berkeley, California, for giving us permission to include "Touching Peace" by Thich Nhat Hanh.

And, we thank Kristin Lems, for permission to include the words to her very upbeat song, "She Gave Herself A Rose," which appears at the end of Chapter 9. It is on compact disc and audiotape, but it is so appropriate for boosting self-esteem that she might have written it specifically for our readers.

—*Ada P. Kahn and Sheila Kimmel*

CONTENTS

PREFACE

Do you want to feel more confident and behave more assertively? Do you want to feel good about yourself? Proud of your body and the way you look? More satisfied with your relationships? More respected on your job? Do you want to like yourself better? Do you want to have more power in your personal and work life?

If the answer to some or all of these questions is yes, you have taken the first step to fulfilling those goals by choosing this book. In *Empower Yourself,* you will learn to boost your self-esteem and sense of personal power. You will learn how to change the way you feel about yourself and how you react to others in both small and large ways.

You will learn how to recognize passive behavior and change it to more assertive behavior to get what you want. You'll learn how to become more equal in personal relationships and how to relieve some of the stresses of your personal, social, and work lives. You'll learn how to stop others from pushing you around.

This book is about becoming your own heroine—to show you how to become a more likable and admirable self.

You'll learn about Womanpower and the four "A" steps toward self-esteem:

1

Awareness
Acceptance
Alternatives
Action

You'll become aware of what has boosted you up in the past and what put you down; how to consider alternatives, choices, and options for yourself; to emphasize the boosters not the squashers; and to take action. You'll learn to bring up your own energy, set realistic goals for yourself, feel comfortable in taking risks, and become empowered to go after what you want. You'll learn to break out of your cocoon and your barriers, understand your "rubber bands" (bounce-back messages from your past that create "stuck spots" for you), and be more powerful.

In *Empower Yourself,* you'll read about common themes that keep coming back to women from their childhoods; from parents, siblings, and teachers; from marriages; and from all whom they encounter as they grow up and grow older. Because relationships between mothers and daughters, and fathers and daughters, are so important in forming our feelings of self-power, we've included a chapter on those topics. And because so many women hear "It's your age" as an explanation for everything from PMS to increasing facial wrinkles, we've included a chapter called "Growing Older, Growing Wiser!"

In every chapter, we've related the experiences of others who have had power squashers much like you may have experienced. The self-esteem boosters these women have learned to use can help you, too. And throughout the book, we've included brief quizzes to help you identify and work on your own squashers and boosters. There are exercises that can help you change negative self-messages to more positive ones. These boosters will help you on your own route toward goal setting, action plans, and admiring yourself as your own heroine after you empower yourself.

INTRODUCTION

If you are one of the lucky women who travels confidently and powerfully along the road of life, you probably had booster messages as you were growing up. Boosters raise your self-esteem and feelings of personal power. But what if you were one of the unlucky ones whose potential personal power was squashed? Squashers push you down like a plunger and erode your self-confidence and self-esteem.

In this book, you will read about how to shed the cocoonlike layers that have held you in, pushed your self-esteem down, and held you back from getting ahead. You will learn about overcoming self-defeating messages from your past that now bounce back, just like rubber bands, and get in your way of moving forward. You will learn how to emerge as a powerful self, take action, and fly free as a butterfly.

You will read some biographical details about your authors, how they learned to overcome the "rubber bands" of their pasts, and how they developed into the women they are now. You will also read many examples of other women's experiences, to which you may relate.

Empower Yourself with Boosters

Some women have a high sense of self-esteem in one aspect of their lives but not in others. For example, some women operate at a high level of confidence and a positive sense of self-worth at work, but not in their personal lives. Other women respect themselves for their homemaking skills, but need boosters when it comes to getting out in the social or work world. Some women feel totally squashed in both worlds. Some lucky ones are confident and powerful in both settings. Which are you?

Regardless of your needs for boosters, this book can help you find—and use—boosters to help you empower yourself. Boosters can help you overcome your squashers. Boosters can help you make the changes you long to make for life. When squashers loom large in front of you, sometimes you can't see over them or get beyond them. Changing the focus from your squashers to your boosters can help you gain power by raising your self-esteem. Emphasizing your own personal boosters can help you empower yourself to meet challenges and seize opportunities presented throughout life, whether you are 16 or 86 years old.

What Does *Womanpower* Mean?

Womanpower is believing "I can do it." It's as simple as that. Womanpower is being able to do what you want to do because you know you are capable and confident enough to follow through. It is believing in *YOU*.

Womanpower is self-esteem, the value you place on all the parts that together make up the whole package of you. Self-esteem is feeling good about *YOU*. Self-esteem enables you to present yourself confidently in all situations. Self-esteem means knowing that you are lovable, able to love yourself and others, and let them love you back. Self-esteem means knowing that you are capable of doing the tasks you pursue, whether at work, in school, or in community activities.

Self-esteem is appreciation of yourself, acknowl-edgment of your inner strengths—the natural re-sources you were born with and those you have learned along the way.

We wrote this book especially for women, although many men may also benefit from a better understand-ing of some of the concepts. We are addressing women specifically because we believe that today's women have a continuing uphill battle to maintain a good sense of self-empowerment on a personal and professional level.

While the women's movement during the 1960s and 1970s opened up many opportunities for women, it also created the seeming contradiction of how women can conduct themselves assertively, competitively, and successfully in business and yet remain feminine in their outlook and behavior. And while the sexual revolution encouraged women to seek equality and enjoy freedom of sexual expression, it brought with it additional responsibilities.

As women moved into the business world, more societal conflicts were piled on them. Many women who wanted to "have it all" found that the daily balancing of love life, family, and a demanding career caused self-doubt and a feeling of lack of power over their own lives.

Many women today want to be tough competitors on the job, good mothers, and sensitive, sharing lovers. Many say they want to do a better job of mothering than their mothers. Others have the addi-tional weight of emotional baggage from their child-hoods. Such baggage may include early recollections of abusive, alcoholic, depressed, or absent parents, sexual or emotional abuse, poverty, abandonment, or being one of many children who grew up thinking "I don't matter."

Events from early life don't have to be really dramatic to lower self-esteem. For example, what do you think being told "You can't carry a tune so just mouth the words" does to a girl's confidence in a grade-school music class? Or in a ballet class when she's told, "You're so tall, stand in the back row. We want the audience to be able to see the short girls!"

For many, the result is a feeling of squashed self-esteem. And low self-esteem involves more than just how you think and feel about yourself. Your level of self-worth affects your physical and mental health, too. Low self-esteem (negative thoughts about oneself) is a major factor in leading to depressive illnesses. For many women, low self-esteem—and depression—are often linked with false boosters: alcoholism, drug abuse, eating disorders, or sexual promiscuity. Often this cycle of problems begins with squashed self-esteem. While quick fixes may help temporarily, they do not raise self-esteem and ultimately will not help you empower yourself. If you can raise your self-esteem—at any age or stage of life—you have a good chance to break a damaging and dangerous cycle.

In 1991, the American Association of University Women reported the results of a survey on self-esteem among girls and boys. They found that while the majority of 9-year-old girls felt confident and positive about themselves, by the time they reached high school, fewer than a third of those same girls felt that way. The AAUW found that many girls emerge from adolescence with a poor self-image, relatively low expectations for life, and much less confidence in themselves and their abilities than boys of the same age.

If self-esteem is low during high school, as the AAUW survey found, then without appropriate boosts, it just won't get any better. As many women move toward young adulthood, middle age, and onward, self-esteem slides down more rungs on the ladder. For others, it moves up.

We have noticed that some women view the end of their childbearing years with self-perceptions of waning attractiveness. They experience this feeling as a further squasher of their self-esteem. And, as women grow older, some feel less useful, less significant, less important than before. As the population ages, and as more women reach middle age and retirement, it is more important than ever to focus on issues of self-empowerment, self-esteem, and self-appreciation. Women can feel better about themselves at *all* ages. And now is the time to learn how to empower yourself.

Why We Wrote This Book for You

We wrote *Empower Yourself* because, like you, we have experienced moments when we felt overcome by a lack of self-esteem and self-confidence. We have struggled with some of the same issues you may face. Consequently, we have gone through our own self-empowerment boosting cycles and developed a philosophy of Womanpower that helps us every day. It can help you, too. In this book, we have incorporated many aspects of our own definitions of Womanpower—ones we've learned both through personal experiences and the experiences of women around us.

Empower Yourself will help you realize and emphasize your own internal strengths, capabilities, and powers. It will enable you to be what you want to be and do what you want to do. You'll learn how to use and adapt our Womanpower Boosting Cycle to help you meet your own personal needs and goals. No matter what our social or economic circumstances, we are all born with the power to develop self-esteem. This fact may be one of the few warranties that come with life. Remember where you put that warranty. It says, *"I'm Me, I'm strong, and I'm powerful."* Keep your warranty in mind. It can help you to meet life's challenges with confidence and success and to make the most of all opportunities.

Sheila: My Squashers and Boosters

I have experienced extraordinary challenges to my self-esteem and turned some big-time power squashers into boosters.

As a young girl, I was popular, smart, attractive, and the best female athlete in my school. My father always told me I could do anything I set my mind to accomplish. I listened to these boosters; they helped me feel strong and capable.

However, nothing I did pleased my mother. She constantly criticized me for being too fat, too sloppy, not clean enough. The "Fat Sheila" message was a squasher. As a result, I have suffered with weight problems all my life.

Then, at age 15, because of a brain tumor in an optic canal, I lost 80 percent of my vision in my left eye and 100 percent in my right eye. I could no longer do what everyone else my age could do. I could no longer be the best athlete or the best student. I didn't think I was attractive anymore. I feared not being popular.

And my beautiful long, curly blond hair was shaved off before the surgery. I went back to school wearing a wig. I felt very self-conscious because of my crooked eyes. I was now very different. I felt frustrated and squashed in all areas of my life. This was a lot for a 15-year-old to bear.

However, I still had determination, drive, strong will, and ongoing boosters my father nurtured me with: "Sheila, you are the best. You have what it takes. You can overcome anything. You are powerful, forceful, and whole. You can be anything you want to be." I finished high school and went to college, constantly fearful of going out on my own. I fed myself squashers. "What if I get lost? What if I can't find my way? How will I finish all my homework? Who will want to date me?"

Gradually I became accustomed to my poor vision even though I hated it and my appearance. But I listened to my dad's boosters and kept driving myself. At the same time, I got the Big Squasher from my mother: "Don't tell anyone about your blindness. People will think less of you if they know." I interpreted that to mean, "Because you don't see as well as others, you are unwhole, incomplete, and imperfect." I became embarrassed about my poor vision and tried to hide it. I was afraid to risk being judged or not liked by others. I especially did not want others to feel sorry for me.

As a result of my dad's boosters, I pulled myself up and moved toward regaining my personal power. I was determined not to let the bad vision get in my way. My own Womanpower helped me through the rough parts of my life. My own struggle motivated me to want to help others. That has been my lifelong task.

In college, I decided to become a rehabilitation counselor so that I could help disabled adults and kids boost themselves and overcome physical or emotional barriers. After seven years of rehab counseling, I returned to school and trained to be a therapist and counselor, which I have been for the last twenty years. I have helped thousands of women (and men) overcome lack of self-confidence and self-esteem during private psychotherapy and group sessions. After several years as a therapist, I decided I wanted to spread my message to more people so I began public speaking, giving workshops and seminars. I've also become a wife, mother, lecturer, and author.

During college, I met my husband of twenty-eight years. I remember feeling scared to tell him "I am legally blind; I can't drive and I read very slowly" because I was afraid he would leave me. Before dating him, I *never* told my boyfriends about my vision problem. Instead I would bluff and make up lies and excuses. But when I knew Freddie was serious about our relationship, I had to tell.

I wish I had known then what I know now about power and strengths—when I felt so afraid, self-conscious, ashamed, and embarrassed about my poor vision. I realized that my mother was ashamed and embarrassed by her "imperfect" daughter. That's why she admonished me—"Don't tell." That was her insecurity talking; I didn't have to "own" her problems. When I realized that, I felt a burden lifted from me. It was so exhilarating to be released from the bonds of my cocoon at last.

I'm proud that even though I've been legally blind for the last thirty-six years, I found my Womanpower and went forward. However, it took some time.

For years, I didn't tell clients or audiences that I couldn't see. But recently I have been telling audiences about my low vision. Now I speak even more dynamically and authentically. Instead of wasting energy being ashamed and embarrassed, and hiding my secret, I use it to interact even more effectively with others. There are no more rubber bands holding me back, or bouncing back to me with self-defeating messages. I've gone from cocoon to butterfly!

I realize what it means to shed the burden of hiding a secret. The "Sheila, you're fat" squasher I got from my mother took its toll. My own perception of my body eventually led to compulsive overeating. However, at the same time, I continued getting boosters from my father: "You're capable and can do anything you set out to do. I love you the way you are." These boosters successfully combatted the "Fat Sheila" message. My husband Freddie also gives me boosters and love. (When I met him, I remember thinking, *He reminds me of my dad, I better hold on to him!*)

Ada: My Squashers and Boosters

There is nothing in my background as dramatic as Sheila's story. And no really big-time squashers such as child abuse, molestation, alcoholism, or absent parents. Nevertheless, just like most of you, I had plenty of squashers, delivered by very well-intentioned teachers, parents, and my older brother.

Now I can identify a few squashers, just as you will learn to do. First, here's one you may think is frivolous: During a grade school singing session, my teacher told me, "You can't sing. Just stand in back and mouth the words." To this day, I am afraid to sing out loud. Little did the teacher realize how she squashed my potential singing ability!

An even earlier one I remember was being referred to as "Little Sister." My brother was three years old when I was born. When I was a toddler, my parents introduced us as, "Jack and his little sister." How do you think this made me feel? I didn't have an identity of my own.

In school, my brother and I had the same teachers—although I had them three years after he did. He was very smart, studious, and always got the top grades in his class. Each year, as I entered a new classroom, the teacher would recognize the family name and greet me with, "I hope you're as smart as your brother." I felt that I had to compete with his record—to please the teachers and our parents. (And there I was, in the back row, mouthing the words to songs while everyone else sang out loud.)

When I was about nine or ten, our mother took a part-time job. My brother and I would walk home from school together at lunchtime. He was in charge of the house at lunchtime and after school. He was old enough and capable enough to turn on the stove; I wasn't. He bossed me around more than I liked. When we played together, if he told me to put the game away, I wouldn't argue. I just followed directions. I suffered criticisms, ranging from, "Why do you wear your skirts so long (or short)" to "You always get your own way." I often felt powerless and would withhold any expression of my interests, even about things as simple as which kind of soup to have for lunch or who should be banker in the Monopoly game. I usually gave in rather than risk starting an argument.

· For years now, my brother and I have been able to talk freely about our early lives and how we got to be the way we are now. He admits bullying me to cover up his own insecurities. He excelled in academic skills, but secretly envied what he regarded as my "people" skills. I seemed to have many friends and a more active social life. His attempts to control me with ridicule and put-downs was his way of compensating for what he thought he lacked: his own self-esteem. But the squashers he dealt eroded some degree of my self-esteem and later kept coming back as self-defeating messages: "I can't do anything right. I'm stupid and dumb. I'm not old enough to know any better."

In the early grades, kids called me "Ada Potata" (ate a potato, get it?) and I hated it. Now that I use the name Ada P. Kahn, even more jokes are possible (e.g., ate a pecan), but now I just laugh and don't mind one bit.

On balance, my boosters must have overcome my squashers. Despite a few unintended squashers my parents gave me, they also left me with many good boosters. They outgrew the "Little Sister" stuff before I did and began calling me Ada. But even then, I felt a little defective in the name game. I lacked something many others had: a name that could be changed into something more affectionate, such as Lizzie for Elizabeth or Florrie for Florence. After all, Big Brother was known in the family as Jackie—to which, I know now, he inwardly cringed. Perhaps my perception of my own somewhat defective name was why I chose to name my daughter Ruth and began calling her Ruthie the moment she arrived.

In general, my parents encouraged me to do what I wanted to do. For example, in sixth grade, I announced that I wanted to enter an American Legion essay contest. In selecting "A Great American" to write about, I ruled out Washington and Lincoln, assuming everyone else would choose them. When I said that I would like to find a woman to write about, they helped me identify Helen Keller, not only a great American, but a powerful and heroic woman who overcame major life obstacles. And I won the first prize. Prizes are big self-power boosters!

In the early 1950s, when I graduated high school, my parents, who were typical of the era, helped to perpetuate the myth of "happily ever after": girls should get married and raise families—and that should be the story of their lives. Still, they supported my decision to bypass the so-called safe fields of teaching and nursing to major in journalism, particularly when a scholarship to a good journalism school came my way. They said that there had been many famous women writers, and Ada could be one, too.

How I Met Sheila

Sheila and I met in the late 1970s when I enrolled in Sheila's assertiveness-training class at Oakton Community College in Skokie, Illinois. We reacquainted in the early 1990s and found that each, in our separate ways, had spent years working with and writing about women and self-esteem. I had written several books on women's health and psychology and directed a hospital-based women's health–education program. Sheila had been teaching groups about self-esteem and doing psychotherapy for years. We decided to share the ideas we had each learned from our work with each other and our readers.

At the time I took Sheila's course, I was on a successful career track, well-respected, with many years of success as a writer and public-relations consultant. When I signed up for Sheila's class, I had come to the realization that on a personal basis, I felt a lack of assertiveness. When facing personal confrontation, I would give in and back away (and at times even dissolve into tears) rather than state what I wanted or believed. In a few short sessions, Sheila taught me how to be more assertive without being obnoxiously aggressive. I learned techniques to overcome anger and frustration and to stand up and speak out for what I believed and wanted.

When I heard about Sheila's assertiveness training class more than fifteen years ago, I realized that I was tired of cringing and caving in. I was a perfect candidate for assertiveness training—a field that wasn't well-known or thought about even a few years earlier. Though I had a fairly good foundation of self-esteem, I also had a mixed collection of old squashers. Be assured that while squashers come in all sizes and shapes, their effects invariably work the same way on self-esteem.

Taking Sheila's course was an important turning point for me. Through working with Sheila, I became more aware and understood my powerless behaviors. I also accepted the fact that I wanted to make changes. I realized that there are always alternatives for handling my personal situations—ranging from standing up to my brother or being more assertive in my marriage to asking for refunds in department stores. I learned to feel more confident and powerful in saying what I wanted to say; learned how to consider my alternatives and take action.

Sheila's course also helped me put my long-ago divorce in perspective. I am now able to look back on my marriage and realize that there were many situations in which I could have been more assertive and powerful. Instead I took a passive, unsuccessful approach. My ex-husband remarried shortly after our divorce, which was a major blow to my self-esteem.

Before the divorce, my husband gave me many small squashers: "You're not the girl I married anymore." "You always . . ." "You never . . ." But I overcame all that. I know I'm a capable and lovable person.

Now, my ex-husband and I get along well. We can talk about our daughter's opportunities, successes, and recent marriage. His current (third) wife and I are good friends. Outsiders compliment the way he and his wife, and I, our daughter and son-in-law interact at family gatherings.

Let Others Look Up to You

I continue to find self-esteem boosters to counteract earlier squashers. For example, I was always the tallest girl; in eighth grade I towered over the boys. Long before anyone else grew, I was 5' 11". My parents always reminded me to stand up straight, but I felt too different from the other girls. In an effort not to stand out even more in a crowd, I was often quiet and passive in social groups.

The best booster I ever got regarding my height occurred in the 1980s while I was writing *Midlife Health: A Woman's Practical Guide to Feeling Good.* The boost came from an interview with the late Anne Rudolph, then a vigorous 78-year-old dancer and instructor in body movement. While we were speaking about the best exercise for flexibility and physical fitness for midlife women, we talked about my posture. Anne Rudolph said, "Stand straight and tall. Let others look up to you." This was the boost I had needed throughout my teen years, and I've used it ever since!

Having grown up feeling self-conscious about my height, I usually dressed conservatively and wore tiny jewelry, to avoid drawing more attention. But Anne's "stand tall" message changed my outlook.

Yet my two biggest boosters came recently, while writing this book. Of course, friends would ask what I was working on and I would mention *Empower Yourself.* One woman, my neighbor and dear friend for the last twenty years, told me, "I'm so glad you're doing this book. I want to learn to be just like you!" And then a new "Significant Man" in my life said he couldn't imagine me being anything but assertive and full of self-esteem. With these boosters, I felt that I had truly graduated from Sheila's class.

Start Right Away Toward Your Goals

We will introduce you to many ways you can begin transforming old negative energy into new self-esteem–boosting messages. We hope to motivate you to start right away, whether your concern is being more assertive, improving a relationship, finding a better job, or getting the raise you want.

Soon you can begin to feel better about yourself regardless of the squashers you've received in life. With each small achievement, you will feel more capable and confident about taking further action, and you'll make even more changes as you meet each new challenge with boosted self-esteem and increased confidence.

1

FIND THE POWER WITHIN YOU

What is empowerment all about? Empowerment is feeling safe and comfortable in expressing what you think; in feeling happy, glad, sad, or angry; in asking for what you want; and in knowing that you have the right to choice, privacy, and respect. For you, empowerment is Womanpower. Womanpower is self-esteem. It is self-confidence. It is being assertive. It is saying NO when you mean no. It is acknowledging your inner strengths and appreciating and admiring your inner self.

With Womanpower, you can be your own heroine and empower yourself.

When you are empowered, you realize that you have the right to please whom you want and dislike whom you choose. You know that you have the right to be the judge of your own behaviors, feelings, and opinions. Does this sound like you? Or does it sound like the way you would like to be?

All people are born with equal potential to become confident and powerful. However, for many reasons, some people, and particularly women, grow up hiding their core selves. They may have unmet needs, unrealized goals, unfulfilled dreams, unsatisfying lives—and, ultimately, they don't feel good about themselves. They don't feel powerful.

Many factors can work together to ruin a young woman's self-esteem. Among the most common are

17

growing up in a family that has unrealistic expectations of perfection in appearance, performance, or
scholarly achievement; or a family that is physically
or psychologically abusive or absent; or in an alcoholic family. A girl who grows up with constant criticism,
without love, or in fear, may want to hide in her own
cocoon forever so that no one can hurt her. A cocoon
feels like a safety net; it's protection from the pain
others may inflict.

What happened to the girls in the American Association of University Women survey who at age nine
were confident but lost their self-esteem by the time
they reached high school? Somewhere along the line
their Womanpower was squashed.

With approval and security, a young woman can
learn to admire and love herself and others, and
develop a high sense of empowerment and self-
esteem.

The following quiz is designed to help you begin to
understand your own style of behavior. You can start
to build your personal workbook with this as the first
page.

WHERE DO YOU STAND ON THE WOMANPOWER SCALE?

Answer each of the following questions with a YES or
a NO. When you have finished, you will be able to
determine where you stand on the Womanpower
scale. Throughout the book, you'll be able to compare
some of your own answers with those of women who
have learned to develop their own power. And as you
work through the self-empowerment program in this
book, you may want to take this quiz again, just to see
how you are improving.

THE WOMANPOWER SCALE

	YES	NO

Do you like yourself?

Are you proud of the way you look?

Do you let people know what you think or feel?

Do you stand up for what you believe in?

Do you ask for what you want?

Do you ask for help when you need it?

Do you let people know when you're unhappy or discontent with their service?

Do you take care of your physical health-care needs?

Do you often put your needs before needs of others?

Do you say no to people who make demands on you without feeling guilty?

Do you recognize your abilities?

Do you live up to your potential?

Do you feel pleased with your career or job decision?

	YES	NO
Are you feeling fulfilled in your present job/school or career track?		
Are you being compensated for what you are worth?		
Do you express your opinions on the job to your superiors?		
Do you initiate new ideas in your workplace or school setting?		
Do you stand up for yourself?		
Do you stop others from putting you down?		
Do you stop people from trying to control your life?		
Do you, as a woman, feel as capable as a man?		
Will you go to a class or program if you can't find anyone to go with you?		
Would you go to a social gathering when you won't know anyone there?		
Can you walk into a social gathering where you don't know anyone and start talking to someone?		
When you're at a social gathering, do you feel like you belong there?		
Are you able to let go of negative experiences?		

                          YES   NO

Do you feel satisfied with
the way you spend your
time?

Are you content with
your choice of partner or
spouse?

If you felt stuck in a
personal situation, have
you been able to pull
yourself up?

Are you able to make
necessary changes in your
life without letting your
fears control you?

How to Score Yourself

If you answered NO to more than 10–15 questions, you may need boosters.

Ask yourself why you answered NO. Are there some circumstances under which you would answer the same question YES? Are there some specific areas of your life in which you would like to boost yourself? As you read through the book, concentrate on the chapters that best address your personal needs.

You are not alone in answering NO to many of the above questions. You are probably among the millions of other women who were bombarded with squasher messages as you grew up. You may also have the combined burden of personal as well as societal squashers.

Some young women get personal squashers from their parents. For example, some hear comments such as, "We hoped to have a boy first, but you came along." Or, "You were an accident. We didn't want another child." Or, "You never do anything right."

While parents may say these things in an off-handed way with no malicious intent, frequent negative comments can have a psychologically damaging effect.

Other young women receive personal squasher messages because absent parents or physical or psychological abuse or overwhelming demands were part of their everyday lives. Young women growing up in these situations may feel unimportant, that their feelings don't matter, and that they exist to be the caretakers for others.

Many women who have reached midlife are aware of another factor that squashed their self-esteem: the societal factor of limited career choices. Women who may have wanted to become lawyers, doctors, or engineers were told when they were younger, "Become a teacher or a nurse. Those are safe fields for women. You'll soon get married and have children anyway, and you won't use your education." Or, "You're so pretty. You'll never have to work. Your husband will take care of you." Many of these women, now in their 50s and 60s, feel that they never lived up to their potential because they were stopped from entering careers they desired. Interestingly, many older women now are entering professional schools, pursuing careers from which they were barred a generation ago, and recapturing their self-esteem.

Although more professional opportunities are available to women now, societal squashers still get in the way. For example, in business today, women may hit a "glass ceiling" (see page 174) in corporate life and feel blocked in moving up the career ladder by something they cannot even explain.

Here are examples of four women whose self-esteem was squashed by outside sources. However, by following our steps toward empowerment, they boosted their self-esteem and their lives today are happier and healthier. Meet Cindy, Bonnie, Susie, and Fran (not their real names).

Cindy: The Woman Who Swallowed Herself

Cindy is now 50 years old. We call her The Woman Who Swallowed Herself because she used to turn to food to boost her feelings of self-worth. As she swallowed food, she swallowed her feelings. This is what she told Sheila during consultation:

> I was the eldest of three children. My mother and father both worked long hours, and I took over responsibilities for caring for my two younger brothers. I often felt like Cinderella; I never had a good time as a child. My parents never hugged or kissed me—they were emotionally and physically distant and unavailable. We were a low-income family, and they couldn't afford to send me to college, although I later managed to go on a scholarship and get a degree in early-childhood education.
>
> When I was 20 years old, I met and married Ron, who was already a successful businessman. He was older and swept me off my feet. It seemed that he loved me and could take care of me. I saw him as my source of escape from my parents. I viewed him as the missing parent figure who could provide affection as well as material things for me. Finally my life seemed good; someone could take care of me rather than require me to be the caretaker.
>
> Early in the marriage, I fed my husband's ego and didn't express my own ideas or desires. Very quickly I observed that Ron was domineering and had macho ideas about marriage and the role of a wife. We had three children. I spent years in the role of caretaker to my family, with little or no help from Ron, who was always preoccupied with himself. In fact, I was repeating the old pattern I wanted to avoid.

*Ron doled out money and asked me to account
for everything I spent. He wouldn't let me work,
even part-time. He constantly put down my interests and opinions. Whenever I enjoyed something, he squashed my feelings of satisfaction.*

*My home was comfortable; Ron provided for
our material wants. But through the years, my
satisfaction with the physical aspect of our relationship waned tremendously. I even suspected he
was having affairs. I live with a hatred of being
constantly repressed by him. I feel no love for him
anymore and want out of the marriage. But other
than deciding to marry him, I never was able to
take a serious step on my own. Now I feel stuck
and scared.*

*For years, the only aspect of my life over which
I felt any sense of control was the food I ate. Food
was a booster for what I lacked and as a result I
became very fat.*

That is why we call Cindy "The Woman Who
Swallowed Herself." We think many other obese
women put food in their mouths, because doing so
gives them a feeling of control and power. For Cindy,
food was also love and comfort, a friend, which filled
the void never filled in her childhood or her marriage.

Do you identify with that feeling? Take a look at
where Cindy stood on the Womanpower Scale. Here's
how she answered some of the same questions you
answered earlier in this quiz.

Looking Inside The Woman Who Swallowed Herself

Do you like yourself?

CINDY: NO. I feel like I don't have a real self. I've
always done what others wanted me to
do. First my parents, then my husband.
I've done things for them and for my
children, but whenever I wanted to do
something for myself, I felt blocked.

Are you proud of the way you look?

CINDY: NO. Just look at me! I have to wear clothes that look like tents!

Do you let people know what you think or feel?

CINDY: NO. I've never been able to do that. My opinions don't seem to matter. I don't think my feelings are important.

Do you let people know when you're unhappy or discontent with their service?

CINDY: NO. I can't even return something that doesn't work.

Do you take care of your physical health-care needs?

CINDY: Sometimes. I'm trying to pay more attention to myself. I know it's not healthy or attractive to be so overweight.

Do you often put your needs before needs of others?

CINDY: NO. That's the way I grew up. My parents as well as my husband expected my wants to come last. If I say no, I feel so guilty. I've always done what was asked of me.

Do you feel pleased with your career or job decision?

CINDY: I never had a career, and every time I tried to do volunteer work I liked, my husband bad-mouthed my choice and I quit. My career was taking care of my parents, my husband, and my children. It's not enough.

Do you express your opinions?

CINDY: As a volunteer at school functions, I was never able to say no when the other mothers asked me, even when I felt overwhelmed by their demands.

Do you stop people from trying to control your life?

CINDY: NO. If I could, maybe I wouldn't have turned to food.

Would you go to a social gathering when you don't know anyone there?

CINDY: Probably not. I'm usually afraid to go anywhere alone. I don't think people will want to talk to me.

Do you feel satisfied with the way you spend your time?

CINDY: NO. My husband criticizes everything I do, to the point where I quit doing things I enjoy.

Are you able to make necessary changes in your life without letting your fears control you?

CINDY: NO. I'm afraid of taking a major step on my own.

Do you identify with some of Cindy's answers? Are you stuck in a position of always saying YES when you would like to say NO? Do you feel that you are stuck in a situation you would like to change? Cindy, like you, needed boosters to counteract some of the squasher messages she received throughout her life.

Here's What Cindy Did

Feeling that her life was being stifled, she began to acknowledge that her only solution was to make some changes. During consultation with Sheila, she accepted the fact that she had followed a pattern that had been set for her by her parents and then Ron. Realizing that she had alternatives, she took some action.

First Cindy began participating in a support group for women seeking divorce at a community-service agency. (At first, she told Ron and the children, now age 8, 10 and 13, that she was going to a weight-loss group.) She met a lawyer she felt she could trust. She confronted Ron with her wish to be out of the marriage. He acknowledged that he too wanted out, and in fact, had a "friend' with whom he wanted to live. (Her suspicions of an affair were correct!) He moved out of their house.

Now it is three years since their divorce. Ron sends money for the children regularly but only sees them about once a month. Cindy took some night-school courses to bring her education up to date and has a job as a nursery-school teacher, which permits her to be home in the early afternoons for the children.

She began an exercise and weight-loss program. Her children do video workouts with her. She plans her meals carefully and is aware of when she is eating to swallow her feelings.

Bonnie the Butterfly

It is possible to use boosters to overcome the squashers one receives in life. Take a look at Bonnie. We call Bonnie "The Butterfly" because she came out of her self-built cocoon.

At 59, Bonnie is a powerful, confident woman in a new career and a new love relationship. But she wasn't always that way.

Here's what Bonnie first told Sheila:

My mother was severely depressed, and this was before the use of antidepressant medications was prevalent. She often spent days in bed, leaving our house in a mess. My father frequently was absent from the home because of his work, and usually sent me to my grandmother's house on weekends because he thought I needed more care than he could provide for me and my two infant brothers.

I loved Grandma, but she was a very controlling person. At Grandma's house, I felt like an outsider who really did not belong there. I really wanted more attention from both my mother and father. I tried very hard to please, win approval, and not get in the way or cause trouble at Grandma's. I just did everything I was told. I thought, if I please everyone and don't make any demands, then everyone will love me.

I remember a time when my mother left me in the hospital, very sick with a high fever, even though I begged her not to leave me. My mother said, "I have to take care of your brothers."

Growing up, I developed an extreme fear of being abandoned. I perceived being sent to Grandma's as abandonment, and my mother's indifference as lack of love. As a child I decided that something must be wrong with me.

I got married when I was 18. Although Dan charmed me during our courtship, he was a dominating man who took little interest in having sex with me. He seemed to fear the closeness that I so desperately needed. About a year after the wedding, he stopped showing any affection or warmth, which reinforced my feeling that I'm defective and unlovable.

I started going out with other men to fill the void in my life, but that wasn't really satisfying because I still came home to the rejection. I wanted to leave the marriage but stayed out of powerlessness, lack of assertion, and fear of aban-

*donment. I knew that Dan would never leave me.
I feared being alone and needed a secure, safe
place because I did not have that as a little girl.
But really, that was a lie. My home and marriage
did not feel safe or secure.*

However, after counseling, and after developing
more Womanpower, Bonnie and Dan attended counseling sessions and group therapy together. He, too,
had problems regarding close relationships, particularly with women. Their sense of communication
with each other has improved 100 percent, says
Bonnie, their love life has improved dramatically,
and they look forward to happily growing old together.

How Bonnie Became the Butterfly She Is

With a series of self-esteem boosting techniques,
Bonnie metamorphosed into a very outgoing, confident, powerfully feminine woman, who now is able
to take necessary steps toward a satisfying life. She
came out of her cocoon.

Bonnie realized that she is a whole and complete
person and that people will like her because of who
she is. She knows she has the right to speak up for
herself, do what she wants, and not put her wishes last
as she had done for so long.

Bonnie now understands that her depressed mother
was a troubled person, and because of the illness,
could not be emotionally or physically available to
her. Bonnie also understands that her father denied
her mother's illness, and acting out of that denial, sent
Bonnie to Grandma, also making himself unavailable
to her.

Once Bonnie understood these truths, she realized
that she wasn't a defective person. She was really okay
and was filled with untapped power and potential.
Once she started taking the first steps toward Womanpower, she became aware of the truths about her

family. She could start breaking out of her cocoon and overcome her self-defeating messages.

Since then Bonnie has taken many major steps toward self-empowerment. She began by acknowledging that she wanted to change her life. She accepted the responsibility for making changes, realizing that she was the only one who *could* change her life. She accepted some truths about herself and her parents, husband, and marriage. She developed the ability to look at alternatives in her day to day activities and make more positive, satisfying choices. She finally became capable of taking actions, based on considerations of alternatives. She even helped her husband— with counseling—to fulfill his potential, and thus their potential together.

Here's how Bonnie answered some of the questions on the Womanpower scale after her metamorphosis:

The Butterfly Self

Do you like yourself?

BONNIE: YES. I have confidence I never had before. I like myself now. I take care of myself. I know I am important, even though my parents and my husband never let me feel that way.

Do you ask for help when you need it?

BONNIE: YES. I know that I deserve help when I need it.

Do you let people know when you're unhappy or discontented with their service?

BONNIE: YES. I'm entitled to. My opinions and need for good service are as deserved as anyone else's and should be respected.

Do you often put your needs before needs of others?

BONNIE: YES. Sometimes it's necessary, and when it is, it's not selfish to do so. Sometimes you have to say no. I can't say yes to everyone and everything.

Are you feeling fulfilled in your present job?

BONNIE: YES. After Dan and I reconciled, I went to a training course for lab techs. My co-workers like me and I enjoy meeting the public. I was even able to ask for a raise after six months on the job.

Do you stop people from trying to control your life?

BONNIE: YES. I'm in control now. I let my parents and husband control me before. I know that some men can do things I can't, but I can do some things that some men can't. It's not a wo-man—man issue. It's an issue of self-esteem.

Would you go to a social gathering when you won't know anyone there?

BONNIE: YES, but I'm still working on that one. There was a time when I rarely felt comfortable in any group. Now I feed myself boosters on the way. I tell myself that I look good, I'm dressed right, that I will be friendly, and people will like me. And they do.

Are you able to make necessary changes in your life without letting your fears control you?

BONNIE: YES. I'm no longer afraid, I know I need security, but I feel confident in making changes. You can see the progress I made with my life as well as my marriage.

What Do Cindy and Bonnie Have in Common?

Cindy and Bonnie both received more squashers than boosters. They both patterned their lives in powerless ways, focusing their attention on their squashers. In looking for ways to pull themselves out of unhappy situations, at first they turned to false boosters. Cindy turned to overeating. Then she accepted the fact that food for her was only a quick fix—a temporary, false booster. She managed to lose some weight and gained the self-esteem to control her eating habits.

For a time Bonnie tried extramarital affairs as a booster. She discovered, however, that over the long haul, sex did not help her. Later she found real boosters in her own self-esteem that worked.

Susie "Should"

In contrast to Cindy and Bonnie, meet Susie, whose parents were very attentive to her needs. However, we call her "Susie Should" because her example illustrates how being talked to with *"you should"* statements causes pressure on a young woman.

Here's what she told Sheila during a group-therapy session:

I'm 31. I was an only child and came from a loving home. My parents were caring, involved, athletic, and appeared to be "perfect" parents. But they had wanted a boy, and made certain to let me know it. You should get top grades, they said. If I didn't get all A's they made me feel very inadequate. They said I should go to a good college and urged me to get an MBA degree. I did, and now I have a good income and an executive management job with a big company. I may look powerful, but I'm not. Sometimes I look in the mirror and say, "This can't be me. I'm what my parents said I should be."

I would have preferred to go into some field of art. I loved to visit art galleries and wanted to paint, but never had time. My parents gave me so much, I couldn't let them down—I felt I should be both their son and *daughter. I believed that I should be like them. I became a business person like my father, but at the same time became very active in women's clubs because that's what my mother did. I thought I should be everything a man could be as well as everything expected of a traditional woman like my mother.*

I filled up every minute of my day with something. I went to work every day because it was expected of me, even though I hated the corporate life. I said yes to all requests from the social organizations I belonged to, but often felt overwhelmed by their demands.

I was afraid I wouldn't be liked by my parents, and later others, if I didn't always say yes. I had convinced myself that I should be everything to all people to be accepted. The combination of a job I disliked, plus the commitments to the women's clubs, made my stress level very high.

Susie's body began to rebel. She often had weeks of not feeling well, pushing herself to go to work and to her social engagements. Then her symptoms became more serious: frequent shortness of breath and bad headaches.

Here's What Susie Did

She took the first step by acknowledging that she was feeling stuck, sick, and that she wanted to make changes for the better.

*Over time I learned that I can be a few things to
some people and still be okay. I dropped the
squasher of I SHOULD from my vocabulary.
And eventually I learned to say no when I wanted
to, and to feel okay about doing so.*

When Susie stopped listening to her "shoulds," she
freed her inner self to pursue her true goals:

*I have a dream of quitting my office job and
opening up my own art gallery. I'm now saving
money so that I can do this. Now that I have
confronted my emotions, I stopped having headaches. I feel better. Before I was living a lie,
according to SHOULD, not to what I truly
want.*

Fran, the Family Fixer

Fran is 29. She is an example of another woman
who grew up with the subtle pressure of SHOULD,
but hers became: "I SHOULD be the FIXER." Here's
the story she told in a group session:

*My parents were good parents for me and my
younger brother. Our home was comfortable. But
my mother was passive, living her life for her
husband and children. My father started drinking
heavily when I was about 10 years old, and it
worsened during my teen years. He was never
abusive or mean, but his drinking worried my
mother a lot.*
*When I was old enough to drive, my mother
would ask me to go to the bar and bring my father
home. My mother expected me to do just what
she herself couldn't do, and manipulated me into
it. I was afraid to leave home to go to college; I
felt I had to save my father from drinking and my
mother from having to cope with his habits. I*

believed that I was responsible for fixing everything and everyone.

When I got married at age 21, I put my parents first, and consequently my marriage failed. My husband couldn't handle the competition. My mother didn't help, with comments like, "You made a bad choice. He's not a good man. I was the one who was always there for you." I was torn between my parents and their needs, and trying to develop a good marriage. I developed an ulcer instead.

Now I'm divorced. I have a pretty good job in a clothing store, even without a college degree, and began to save some money. I learned to ease my frustrations through artistic expression, by making jewelry, which I now sell at a very high markup in boutiques.

Two years ago, my mother became ill with severe arthritis. As a result, she can no longer drive. I had to quit my sales job to meet her obsessive demands. Then my father had a stroke that disabled him. My mother couldn't take care of him because of her arthritis. So I asked my parents to move in with me in my small apartment, and I became their full-time nurse. The income from the jewelry plus their social security checks was enough to get us by.

Then a friend said, "What about you? You're saving your parents, but your ulcer is getting worse. You can't date because you are afraid of leaving them home alone. That's no life for a young woman."

How Fran Changed Her Life

Fran looked at her own life and accepted the fact that the situation she was in was largely one she had chosen. She finally got to the point where she was able to consider alternatives to her overwhelming situation. She could put her parents in a nursing home or hire a full-time nurse-homemaker. When she told her parents about the alternatives she was considering, her mother tried to make her feel guilty.

However, finally, Fran summoned up the power to take a step forward and found a full-time live-in homemaker to take care of her parents in their own home. She would supervise the homemaker situation from a distance. Her ulcer got better. She's off of medication. She is able to have a social life of her own.

Fran's story illustrates a theme common in many women's lives: the caretaker role. It's hard to break out of that role, at any age. Fortunately for Fran, she has realized that she is really no good to anyone if she doesn't take care of herself first—at least some of the time.

2

MEET YOUR SQUASHERS
HEAD-ON AND GAIN POWER

Squashers are like rubber plungers that push down your self-esteem until you can't find it. Or they may work like the waves on a rocky coastline, which cause erosion and change the profile of the landscape.

Squashers are messages that cause you to feel less worthy than other people. Squashers are put-downs. And like rubber bands, they cause a "bounce-back" effect later on. A rubber-band response is when you overreact to something or someone in a way that is way out of proportion to the situation. It's a bounce back to a time when you *really* experienced the squasher. For example, someone may have said to you that you were wearing the wrong kind of clothes for an important party. Later, when another person comments on the way you look, you may feel as badly and as squashed as the first time a similar comment was made.

You may hear criticism in a statement when it was not intended. You may misinterpret and overreact, get angry and defensive, just the way you did to your parents, a teacher, or another child when you were younger.

Understanding that squashers can bounce back against you and put you down is a step toward overcoming them. You need to be able to identify your old squashers and replace them with new boosters, otherwise you will continue to give yourself negative or self-defeating messages. Squashers and rubber-band messages are part of your "shell." They keep you in your cocoon. Boosters help you get out.

Negative Self-Talk Defeats You

For many women, self-esteem squashers from childhood, adolescence, and even adulthood result in negative self-talk. The degree to which women function effectively and confidently later in life depends to a large extent on the kinds of messages they received along the way. However, squashers continue to be around us all through adulthood, too. If you are vulnerable enough, you'll hear many things in adult life that can layer more squashers on you. The effects of squashers received in adulthood are the same as those received in childhood: They result in negative self-talk that requires conversion to boosters for you to empower yourself.

For many women, common early squashers may have included having an overly critical parent or teacher, having a poor body image—being called "fatty," or "toothpick"—being foreign born, being the school scapegoat, being the youngest child and told "you don't matter," simply being a girl, or being told "you're just a pretty face." For some women, more serious squashers may have included having alcoholic, abusive, or depressed parents, or feeling abandoned.

Squashers can come from parents, teachers, siblings, spouses, or friends. Some people may barrage you with squashers for no reason at all—or for the simple reason that they had a bad day at work and are taking out their frustrations on you. Some people send squashers to you without even realizing they do it.

Then there are indirect squashers, such as guilt. For example, a parent may ask a child who gets three A's and one B on a report card: "What about that B?" That squasher ignores the three A's and focuses on the one B. The child then feels worthless about her accomplishments and that she just doesn't measure up to her parent's standards.

Whatever the reason you got your squashers, they hurt. The squashers that were layered on you over the years are particularly hard to shed because young people are impressionable and vulnerable.

What Were Your Personal Squashers?

Think about your own personal squashers. How did they start? Begin as far back as you can remember. Think about anyone to whom you were exposed or from whom you heard what you interpreted as a put-down. When layered over the years, squashers and put-downs cover up your core, powerful self.

In this chapter, you will begin to shed layers of the cocoon under which your self-esteem may be hiding. You will learn ways to change old squashers to new power boosters. You can use boosters to work head-on against your personal squashers to start pulling up your self-esteem.

As you proceed toward your goal of Womanpower, here's a quiz to help you identify your personal squashers.

WHERE DO YOU STAND ON THE SQUASHER (POWERLESS) SCALE?

Answer the following questions with YES or NO. More than 10 YES answers equals a high squasher score, which means that you need to work on boosting your squashers.

THE SQUASHER SCALE

	YES	NO

Do you often put yourself down?

Do you often worry about what might happen?

Do you overreact to situations?

Do you blow things out of proportion?

Do you often find fault with yourself?

Do you often find yourself noticing mistakes you make?

Do you criticize yourself often?

Are you ashamed of the way you feel?

Are you ashamed of the way you look?

Does it take major effort to make you feel happy?

Do you discount your own accomplishments?

Do you often hide your accomplishments from others?

Do you have difficulty accepting compliments?

Do you let others push you around?

Are you often intimidated by others?

                              YES   NO

Do you usually put others
first?

Do you shrivel up when
faced with confrontation?

Do you avoid confrontation
because you are afraid of
the consequences?

Do you scare easily?

Do you often feel that
others are better or
smarter than you?

Do you often stop
yourself from saying what
you want because you are
afraid of the negative
consequences?

Do you often feel jealous
of others?

Do you wish you were
somebody else?

Do you let others make
choices for you?

Do you say yes when you
want to say no?

Do you hold back your
feelings because you are
afraid of what others will
think?

Are you ashamed of your
feelings?

Do you get embarassed
easily?

Do you hold back your
anger for fear of the
consequences?

	YES	NO
Do you often feel frustrated and resentful?		
Do you get mad at yourself easily?		
Do you feel stuck in a rut and afraid to make a change?		
Do you stay stuck because you're afraid of failure?		

Identify Your Boosters and Squashers: The Squasher-Booster Profile

By examining your answers to the above quiz, you will begin to identify some of your own squashers. When you recognize your negative self-messages and learn how to find complementary boosters to counteract the put-downs, you will be able to draw up your personal Squasher–Booster Profile. Then you will create positive messages that fit in your own Personal Booster Basket at the end of this chapter. (Don't peek yet.)

The following chart gives examples of some common self-esteem squashers and boosters.

SAMPLE SQUASHER-BOOSTER PROFILE

SQUASHERS (I TELL MYSELF)	BOOSTERS (I TELL MYSELF)
I don't belong here.	I belong here.
I'll be left behind.	I'll be included.
I better be good or no one will love me.	I am lovable.

I should be quiet and be careful not to disturb or displease or they won't love me.	I can be Me. I can express my feelings even if they are different from others.
I'm stupid. I'm not smart enough.	I'm smart. I am smart enough and I know a lot.
I'm too fat.	I'm lovable the way I am.
People don't believe me.	I'm believable. What I have to say is important.
I can't.	I can. I can do this one way or another.
I can't do this alone.	I can do this myself.
It will never work.	It will work. I'll figure it out.
I'm afraid of being wrong.	So what if I make a mistake?
I'll make things worse.	Things will get better.
What is wrong with me?	I'm okay.

Boosters That Helped Cindy

Here's another example of a Squasher–Booster Profile. In Chapter 1, you met Cindy, The Woman Who Swallowed Herself.

As a child, I got little attention from my parents. I spent a lot of time taking care of my two little brothers, with little thanks from my parents. They couldn't afford to hire outside help, and I felt used. The only thing I thought I had control over was what I ate. I began to associate giving myself food with giving myself love that I didn't get elsewhere. Later, when I was upset with my

*husband, and even my own children, I would eat
to make myself feel good.*

Squashers Cindy heard as a child:

You're not important.
You don't matter.
Be invisible.
Stay out of the way.
Take care of others.

Cindy combined some of the squashers and told
herself that if she stayed fat, she would be noticed.

While working on the Womanpower Boosting
Cycle (see page 68), here's what she learned about
herself:

CINDY'S SQUASHER–BOOSTER PROFILE

SQUASHERS	BOOSTERS
I can't make decisions myself.	I can made good decisions.
I'm fat.	I'm okay. I can dress attractively.
I better not say no. They won't like me.	I can say no to what and whom I choose. People will like me anyhow.
I'm afraid to go to a social event alone. I'm invisible; no one notices me.	I mix well with a group. I am important. People enjoy talking with me.

Boosters That Helped Bonnie

Also in Chapter 1, you met Bonnie, the one we call
The Butterfly. Here is Bonnie's Squasher-Booster

Profile. Remember, she felt that she didn't matter because her father often sent her to her grandmother's house during her mother's depressive spells. Bonnie felt deprived of her mother's love and nurturing and felt abandoned by both her mother and father. At her grandmother's, she tried hard to please so she would be loved.

During childhood, Bonnie received squasher messages from her mother:

Don't bother me.

I can't take care of you now.

Go away and leave me alone.

Don't touch me.

As a girl, and even as an adult, those squashers were repeated by her inner voice. The chart below shows her internal negative messages and the boosters she used to counteract them.

Bonnie, using the Womanpower Boosting Cycle described in this book, managed to break free from her old patterns of negative thinking. First she realized that she was indeed a lovable person. Next she accepted the fact that her mother had problems and that she had to separate her own self-concept from her mother's problems. She learned to work through a lot of her anger, so she could get on with her life. Her new decision was, "I'm okay. My mom had problems. She is a separate person from me."

BONNIE'S SQUASHER—BOOSTER PROFILE

SQUASHERS	BOOSTERS
I get no response from my mother.	I'm really an okay person. My mother is emotionally unstable.

SQUASHERS	BOOSTERS
I have to constantly be good and perfect to win approval at Grand-mother's house so I will be liked.	I can be me. I'm likable and lovable.
If I don't please others they won't love me and will leave me.	I am capable and lovable. I want to please others because I care about them and not because I'm afraid of losing their love
I'm always scared of doing something wrong.	I can do what I think is right without worrying about what they think.
I'm not important. Something must be wrong with me.	It's okay if I do what I want. I can make mistakes. I don't have to be perfect.

Sheila and Her Squashers

Sheila received some major squashers during her teen years. However, her worst negative message came after many years of boosters from her father; that's why she coped so well in adulthood. Here's how she composed her profile:

SHEILA'S SQUASHER–BOOSTER PROFILE

SQUASHERS	BOOSTERS
Your eyes are crooked; always wear your glasses so no one will notice.	So what if my eyes are crooked? It's what's inside that matters.
You're not attractive.	I look okay. People will like me anyway.
You won't be able to keep up in school.	I'm smart and will work hard to do all the assignments everyone else does.

Don't go out alone because everyone will stare.	I meet new people when I go out alone.
You're fat.	I'm attractive and lovable.
Can't you ever get it right?	It's okay to make mistakes and be imperfect.
Don't tell clients or audiences that you can't see; they won't respect you.	I'm professional and competent. They will respect my profiency even if they know about my low vision.

Ada's Squashers and Boosters

Ada's negative messages came during childhood and early high school. Boosters from her parents and some of her teachers helped her overcome them.

ADA'S SQUASHER–BOOSTER PROFILE

SQUASHERS	BOOSTERS
You are just "Little Sister."	I'm Ada. I'm important.
Your brother is smarter.	I am smart. I am capable.
What you have to say is unimportant.	I have good ideas and my opinions are important.
Don't be assertive; people won't like you.	I can stand up for what I want and think.
You're too tall.	I'm attractive and people like me.
You're too skinny.	It's okay to be thin.

Now that you have read profiles of other women as well as the authors', it's time to draw up your own chart. You may want to use the results of previous quizzes to define your boosters and squashers and then decide which ones you want to focus on.

SELF-TEST: MY PERSONAL SQUASHER–BOOSTER PROFILE

Now it's time to create your own list of personal squashers and boosters. Here are some examples of squashers and boosters. You'll probably select some of these and think of more to add for your own list.

SAMPLE SQUASHERS AND BOOSTERS THAT MAY WORK FOR YOU

SQUASHERS	BOOSTERS
You're too fat.	I look great.
You'll never be able to lose weight.	I can say yes when I want to. People will like me either way.
Say yes so people will like you.	I can be me. I have feelings and opinions, needs and wants. I count.
Be good. Be nice. Be quiet and don't make a scene.	I have the right to express my feelings. My feelings matter.
It's your fault.	I'll make it work.
You're always getting in the way.	I'll figure out a way.

There must be something wrong with you.	I'll face this head-on.
Why can't you be more like . . .	I'll figure out what to say and do.
You're stupid.	I can handle it.
Why can't you be like your sister?	I am bright.
They said I don't have any brains.	I can't control what others do—or say.
They said "You owe me" and "After all I've done for you . . ."	I am responsible for myself. I will tell others what I think and feel.
You can't do it as well as a man.	No one can tell me what to do unless I let them.
Men get all the breaks.	I will make my own choices.
You're weak, a typical woman.	I will turn to others when I want to.
You drive like a woman.	I will ask for what I want.
You think like a woman.	I will say no when I want to.
They'll laugh at me.	I am proud of my opinions, thoughts and feelings.
I won't be able to handle it.	I deserve respect.
Others can do it better.	I have personal rights.
Others are smarter.	I am lovable and likable.
You'll be rejected.	I belong here.

SQUASHERS	BOOSTERS
You'll be sorry.	I'm fun to be with.
Why try; it'll make things worse.	I'm a great friend.
It won't work, anyway.	I can take risks.
That's my luck.	I can accomplish things.
I'm not good enough.	I appreciate my strengths.
You never do things right.	I am a survivor.
You always screw things up.	
You never know what to say.	
You don't deserve it. Other people are better.	

How Squashers Keep You from Empowering Yourself

Power Squashers Come from all Around Us

Do you know any parents who wanted a boy for their first child and had a girl instead? Are you one of them? Some parents tell their daughters about this— all their lives! It makes some girls grow up thinking that they weren't really wanted. Then there are girls who have been told by their parents that they were an "accident." Or that they were adopted because their birth mother did not want them. What does that do to the girl's self-esteem?

Some parents who wanted a boy give their girl a boy's name—or at least a gender-ambiguous name, like Joey, Devon, or Marvyn! This gives a negative message to the girl early on. She either tries to be like a boy and doesn't quite make it, or gives up totally and settles for feeling unwanted.

Parents Who May Fear Your Failure

Being the victim of an anxious mother or father also can layer many squashers upon a young woman. Have you heard any of the following?

Don't go swimming—I will worry too much.

Don't enter the race—you might not win.

Don't sign up for the course—you might fail.

That sport's not for you—you don't have the training.

You can't do this right—I'll show you how. I can do it better.

In many cases, these messages, which show how the parent feels, squash the young person's whole, core self. For example, in the cases of a young person wanting to try something new, the parent's discouraging words may really reflect the parent's fear of *personal* embarrassment if the child does not succeed. Or the parent may fear that the child's achievements will overshadow their own. Or the parent may be genuinely concerned that you might be hurt and that they will be helpless to do anything about it.

If squashers of this type were layered on you, take a kindly attitude while trying to understand their origins. It may not be true that your parents thought you were incapable. Maybe your parents viewed whatever you did as a reflection on them. And they may have been more concerned with *their* own feelings than yours. They didn't want the worry, the shame, or personal embarrassment if you didn't succeed.

Guilt as a Squasher

How many of you have heard comments like these:

If you cared about me, you'd do what I want you to do.
If you loved me, you would . . .
After all I've done for you . . .
You owe me . . .

Guilt is like a ball: When it comes your way you can choose to catch it or not. Don't let the guilt get into your hands. Remember how Bonnie felt? She had to please her grandma when she was there. She believed that if she did everything she was told, others would love her. You are an individual with your own needs, wants, and desires. You can express love and appreciation without letting your true self be completely submerged by another. Many women develop lifelong habits out of guilt. Have you fallen into an unhappy pattern because you feel that you should?

Behavior Patterns That Squash Power

Negative, self-defeating messages can drag down your self-esteem and make you feel powerless. Now you know that squashers are imposed on you from outside—but you may be putting squashers on yourself, too. Self-imposed negative messages include fears, phobias, panic, anxieties, anger, frustration, and "catastrophizing"—the statement you say to yourself that begins "What if?" and ends with the worst-case scenario.

Do you recognize any of these squashers in yourself?

Many women are fearful because they grew up with messages that encouraged fear. Fear blocks potential and causes incapacitation. Fear can make you feel "different" from others, and in doing so, you have less self-esteem.

Wendy the Water Phobic

Wendy is a successful 20-something advertising executive. She excels at her work but thinks less of herself because of her fear of water. "I grew up with my mother telling me, 'Don't go near the water. If you fall in, you might drown.' I interpreted these messages to mean that the water can hurt me. I never take vacations with friends in areas where there is likely to be any lake, river, or large body of water. I think I'm not as good as other people who can go swimming or boating. I think less of myself because I feel 'stuck.' I would love to go on a vacation with some of my friends who enjoy being near water. I feel cut off from an experience my friends can enjoy."

Of course, some children—and adults—actually do experience near-drowning episodes. For them, overcoming the fear of water may be a deeply rooted situation and require work with a psychotherapist. But most people experience fear as a feeling of uneasiness that comes as a normal response to a perceived threat that may be real *or* imagined. Fear is, of course, an appropriate response to a concrete, real, knowable danger. A phobia, on the other hand, is a fear that has been exaggerated totally out of proportion to the threat, and one that is not perceived as a threat by others.

For Wendy, just thinking about large bodies of

water produces an intense, irrational fear. She realizes her anxiety is out of proportion to any potential danger. It cannot be explained or reasoned away, is largely beyond her voluntary control, and leads her to avoid even being near water.

Phobias stop people from doing what they want to do and often result in avoidance of the feared situation. But phobias can be overcome with the help of psychotherapists, behavior modification techniques, and, in some cases, adjunctive prescription medications. And boosters can help affirm what one learns during therapy.

Aggie the Agoraphobic Woman

Aggie is an example of a woman with a debilitating mental-health condition that impairs her activities of daily living as well as her self-esteem. Aggie has agoraphobia, which is more common for women than for men. According to psychiatrists, agoraphobia is really a *fear* of fear. Aggie is afraid to go out alone and be in a variety of situations because she is afraid of being afraid.

> *I'm a 42-year-old wife and mother, and I feel that I am missing out on life. Sometimes I have experienced panic attacks and I'm afraid that I will embarrass myself publicly by panicking where others can see me, and in a place that doesn't seem safe to me.*

Recurring panic attacks are sudden upsurges of acute, intense fear or anxiety, often associated with frantic urges and attempts to escape. Aggie experiences extreme fear, to the point at which she sometimes feels she will suffocate or die if she can't get to a safe place or out of the situation that produced the panic attack.

Aggie is very self-conscious. She knows that her fears are unrealistic. She feels inadequate, as though she just can't handle going to most places or being with people. She lacks confidence and needs to trust herself—to know that she can do it—and to feel empowered to overcome her panic attacks. Agoraphobia is a condition that can be overcome with the help of psychotherapy, behavior modification, and in some cases, with medication.

One frequently successful technique is called *in vivo* therapy, in which the individual learns to cope with one new step at a time in a real-life situation. Learning to use relaxation techniques while facing the feared situations may also help. These techniques can also be helpful for people who have less extreme fears.

Differences Between Phobias and Anxieties

Although many women experience vague feelings of anxiety they may not know *why* they feel anxious. Fear and anxiety differ in intensity but not quality. Anxiety is a vague sense of uneasiness or apprehension, an anticipation of impending doom that has a relatively unspecific source. For some women, anxieties are related to feelings of low self-worth and the fear that others will look down on them.

For example, Cindy, whose mother was severely depressed, was always anxious about bringing friends home, fearing others would think less of her because her mother was often in bed all day long.

Anxiety often arises from low self-esteem and from self-doubt. There seems to be a vicious cycle occurring here: self-doubt leads to worry, which leads to anxiety, which reduces self-esteem, which increases self-doubt—and round and round again.

Anger: An Energy Drain

Angry women may appear to have a sense of high self-esteem; however, the truth is that some women become angry as a hostile reaction to being squashed by another's unfairness or unintended discrimination. Expressions of anger vary from mild irritation all the way to seething rage and violence.

Not too long ago, it wasn't considered feminine or ladylike for a woman to express her anger. Many women either suppressed their anger or expressed it indirectly. Neither behavior is healthy. As more women realize their power and acknowledge that it is okay to express anger, some go to the extreme of expressing anger in a very aggressive way. They may have held in their rage for so long that when they release it, it is all out of proportion to the situation—and it then becomes abusive anger. Passive, passive-aggressive, and aggressive anger are all unhealthy and use up excess energy. Misdirected anger is a squasher because the physiological effects of anger can detract from a woman's overall good health.

In Sheila's case, her anger manifested as rebellion against her mother's constant remarks about being too fat, even when Sheila was really thin.

Here's what Sheila says:

> *I took out my anger toward my mother on myself by overeating. I told myself I was rebelling, but I was really hurting myself by getting fat.*

Repressing anger can result in tension in the body, bringing on stomachaches, headaches, backaches, and other stress-related ailments. There can be physical or emotional pain. You may need to give yourself permission to express your anger instead of internalizing it. Healthy expressions of anger can help you empower yourself; holding in anger can only entrap you.

Catastrophizing Gets in the Way of Empowerment

Catastrophizing is imagining the worst will actually happen." Someone with low-self esteem may believe that an embarrassing moment will cause them humiliation. Such pessimistic thinking prevents many women from taking risks and risking changes.

Here's how Aggie feels:

If I have a panic attack in the supermarket, people will think I am crazy.

If I throw up in public, people will be revolted.

If they see me getting weak and faint, they will think I have some terrible illness.

These are catastrophizing statements. These imagined negative outcomes cause Aggie to avoid potentially fulfilling situations because she fears the worst. They may cause feelings of powerlessness that result in non-productivity. Because she listened to her own negative statements, Aggie remained agoraphobic, unable to leave her house and afraid of having panic attacks. She feels totally debilitated and worries that she is wasting her life.

Catastrophizing includes using self-defeating messages that block us, keep us stuck and immobilized, afraid to make changes. While you may think Aggie is an extreme example, many of us catastrophize over situations that may seem minor to others. We predict that the new, the unknown, the change, the risk, will turn out badly. For example, we may tell ourselves, "I won't go if I can't find a friend to go with me. No one will talk to me. I'll be alone, and I'll feel bad." Or, "I won't accept the invitation to the formal dance. I don't dance well and people will laugh at me."

Learn to Consider Possible Positive Outcomes

Now is the time to start thinking about Possible Positive Outcomes. A Possible Positive Outcome (PPO) is when you tell yourself the good things that could happen if you allow yourself to take a risk or make a change. It is the opposite of a self-defeating message. PPOs are the self-esteem boosters that replace self-defeating messages.

From her school days, Ada recalls:

*When the public speaking teacher said in front of
the class that I was "phlegmatic" and a "broom-
stick," those were squashers. These were the
squashers that led to my self-defeating message of
"I am not a good speaker." Later I learned to
replace these with: "I am an effective speaker and
know my material. I can improve the expression
in my voice and sound good. I can do a good job.
I make a good appearance. I present myself well.
My appearance is fine. I'm really not skinny anymore."*

Aggie, with the help of her therapist, as well as our
self-help techniques, can give herself some boosters,
too:

I can start by going to the supermarket for just
five minutes with a friend.
I'll get on a bus with a friend.
I'll go to the bakery around the corner alone.

Aggie can select the easiest task, such as going to the
bakery, as her first attempt to overcome her phobia.
After she feels comfortable going there, she can attempt her next most-difficult risk, which may be going
somewhere a little farther alone.
Instead of focusing on negative self-talk, and self-
defeating messages, learn to approach situations with
the understanding that there is always a 50 percent
chance of a Possible Positive Outcome. Think about
how just having a Possible Positive Outcome in mind
can encourage you to take action.
Right now, stop and think of at least five PPOs that
you can tell yourself that relate to situations you are
afraid of changing, projects you put off doing because
you fear failure, or people you'd like to see but fear
rejection by them.

Perfectionism, Frustration and Powerlessness

Are you trying to live up to your own expectations? The expectations of others? Are they realistic? Feelings of powerlessness and victimization often lead to frustration. Frustrations are squashers. Frustration may come from unfair and unrealistic demands, e.g., from parents as well as society. Internal frustration may also come from the unrealistic expectations we place on ourselves.

Overcoming pefectionism can be a way to overcome frustration and self-directed anger, particularly obesity, according to Dorothy Young Riess, M.D., past president of the Pasadena Medical Society. "Many women are perfectionists. They set up impossible goals and expect a perfect household, a perfect marriage, perfectly well-behaved children, and a perfect body. When none of these goals are reached, the response is self-criticism and negative thinking. Life is not perfect. We are imperfect human beings. We make human errors. Get rid of the perfection ideal, once and for all."

Dr. Riess has developed some suggestions for overcoming perfectionism, and they are helpful ways toward empowering yourself. Here they are:

- Praise yourself for every little accomplishment.
- Constantly reinforce the positive aspects of your life.
- Allow the negative to slide away by not paying attention to it.
- Remember, positive is powerful!

Lighten Up!

Consider the power of humor in your life. In many cases, humor can lighten the burden of embarrassment or shame. Here's how Sheila handles humor:

My low vision has led to many situations in which a laugh covered embarrassment for me and for others. I call some of these events my "McGooisms." I tell some of them during my motivational presentations.

The Day Sheila Became Stuck in Cement

I was wearing nice new shoes and walking on a downtown Chicago street to meet my husband for lunch. I saw a big orange truck but thought nothing of it. I took a step and realized that my foot was stuck in wet cement. A construction man shouted at me: "Hey lady, didn't you see this huge truck?" "No, I said. Sorry, I don't see well." He hosed down my shoe and we had a laugh together. I went on to meet my husband. "Guess what happened, Fred!"

"You don't have to tell me, you stepped in the wet cement. I thought about waiting for you outside and warning you, but I thought you would see the huge orange truck."

We laughed together.

Ada's Smashing Entrance

Anyone can have a mishap that can be embarrassing and make one feel like crawling under the carpet (instead of falling over it).

Here's one Ada tells:

I was at a meeting in San Francisco and was called to the stage to receive an award from the president of the American Medical Writers Association. In my excitement, I didn't notice the step just before I approached the president at the podium. I caught my toe and went down face-first. In that moment, I envisioned myself coming up bloody, in front of 400 people. The president reached out and grabbed my arm. I managed to reach out to the floor and break the fall with my other arm. How embarrassing. What could I do? What could I say? What did I say? I stood up, straighened my skirt and suit jacket, and said, "This is known as making a smashing entrance." The audience applauded and laughed, and I laughed with them.

Recently, when I told a fellow AMWA member that I was working on a self-esteem book, she said: "You certainly have a lot of self-esteem. I can't think of a better response than the one you made the day you made the smashing entrance."

Know Yourself, Boost Yourself, Like Yourself

Now's the time to fill your Personal Booster Basket. These boosters will help you become more aware of your own strengths and overcome your squashers. You'll want to look into this basket again and again as you read the following chapters.

MY PERSONAL BOOSTER BASKET

Fill in the blanks with as many endings for each statement as you can

My strengths are _____

_____

The aspects of my personality I like best are _____

_____

I am proud of _____

_____

What I appreciate about me is _____

_____

The physical features I like best about myself are ___

_____

My accomplishments are _____

_____

Ways in which I take care of myself are _____

_____

Risks I have taken with successful outcomes are ___

_____

The personality qualities that make me likable are

_____

_____

What others have told me they admire about me are

_____

_____

Difficult life situations I have lived through, handled, and survived are _____

_____

When I feel powerful I can _____

_____

Meet Your Squashers Head-on

By now you have started to develop a new awareness about yourself and the ways you can change how you think and feel about yourself. In this chapter, you have taken a giant step toward empowering yourself by understanding what we mean by:

- Boosters
- Squashers
- Rubber-band messages that snap back to past ideas that hurt you now
- Self-defeating messages
- Possible Positive Outcomes

In the next chapter, you will learn to adapt to your own life the four "A" steps toward Womanpower.

3

LIVE YOUR DREAM:
GET OUT OF YOUR COCOON

Are you ready to live your dream? Think about the areas in your life that you'd like to change. Where would you like to begin? This chapter will help get you moving toward a very important turning point.

Before you can apply the four "A" steps of the Womanpower Boosting Cycle, you'll need to determine what your "stuck spots" are, what specific squashers keep you stuck, and how to free yourself.

Get Going, Get Unstuck and Live Your Dream!

Do you feel that something is holding you back from going toward what you want? Do you feel stuck? What holds you back? What do you want from your life? For each woman, desires vary. For example, one woman desperately wants to lose 25 pounds, another wants to stop smoking, another wants to ask for a raise, and another wants a loving relationship.

The first step in getting yourself "unstuck" is to identify what you want, why you stop yourself from having it—your squashers—and decide which boosters you need to help get you on your way. When you know your squashers, you can meet them head-on with boosters and then go beyond them.

The following exercise will help you get started. Take a piece of paper and follow the sample. When you finish the exercise, keep the page(s) to begin your Personal Workbook. As you read on, keep adding to your Personal Workbook; it will provide a map of your progress toward Womanpower.

AREAS OF MY LIFE I WANT TO BOOST

Head the left-hand column
"MY WANTS"

Head the right-hand column
"MY SQUASHERS"

Make a list of your wants—those things that would make you feel happier, more powerful, and more successful. Write them in the left-hand column. For example:

I want:

- To lose 25 pounds and feel good about my body
- To be able to stand up and give a talk about my hobby
- To ask for a raise

As you list your wants, think about the self-defeating messages that keep you from going after them. How does that make you feel? Now list your squashers in the right-hand column, opposite your wants. For example, squashers for the above wants may be:

- I'll probably never be thin, so why should I bother?
- I'll make a fool of myself; people might laugh.

• I'm afraid I'll get fired if I ask for a raise.

Find Your Own Personal "Stuck Spots"

There are many reasons why you may feel powerless to go after what you want. Reasons differ among women and each woman has a "stuck spot" somewhere that limits her.

Your "stuck spot" is the gap between what you want and how hard you are trying to get it; how important your desire is and the amount of energy you put into it. When stuck, you feel angry, frustrated, depressed, and unable to move forward. For example, your negative messages might be denigrating your internal strengths and resources—thereby holding you back from getting what you want.

How you happened to land in your stuck spot depends on your squashers. They may be getting in your way right now. Do the following quiz, using the examples, to determine the strength of your "stuck spots" and which ones you need to work on.

HOW TO FIND YOUR PERSONAL "STUCK SPOTS"

Rate each of your wants in terms of how important it is to you (Scale of 0–10, with 10 being the most important). Then rate each want in terms of how much energy you are giving it now (Scale of 1–10, with 10 being the most energy).

The formula: Importance − Energy = your Stuck Spot

Example: Judy

WANT	IMPORTANCE	ENERGY	STUCK SPOT
To lose 25 pounds	10	3	7
To speak in front of people about a hobby	9	3	6
To ask for a raise	8	1	7
To start my own business	10	3	7

Example: Louise

WANT	IMPORTANCE	ENERGY	STUCK SPOT
To stop smoking	10	10	0
To complete a night-school project	10	10	0

Louise has a 0 stuck spot regarding her desire to stop smoking. She has been attending a "stop smoking" clinic regularly and has made the commitment to stop. She hasn't had a cigarette in three months. Being able to control her habit instead of the habit controlling her has given her a boost.

Louise also has a 0 stuck spot about her night-school project. She completed a major project after long procrastination. She is proud of herself.

However, Judy seems to have stuck spots regarding losing weight, public speaking, asking for a raise and starting her own business. She needs boosters!

Look at your own stuck spots. Pat yourself on the back for any 0 scores or scores that are low. Don't you feel powerful and successful? Consider that you've given yourself boosters! Once you have realized what you have accomplished, you can go on to tackle more of your goals and dreams!

Where you have the largest stuck-spot scores, think about your squashers. How do you feel about the difference between what you want and what you are doing to achieve it? Do you feel frustrated, angry, depressed? In the next section, you will use the four "A" steps of the Womanpower Boosting Cycle to help you reduce your stuck spots, go after what you want, and feel better about yourself and what you are doing. Remember, no one can do it for you. You are the only one who can make these changes. Before you begin the Womanpower Boosting Cycle, start from a position of strength and power. Don't wait until you are so depressed that it immobilizes you. Think about:

- Risks you have taken
- Accomplishments you are proud of
- Wants you have achieved

The Womanpower Boosting Cycle: The Four "A"s

Here are the four steps of the Womanpower Boosting Cycle:

- AWARENESS
- ACCEPTANCE
- ALTERNATIVES
- ACTION

The steps move from one into the other in a circular way. They feed into each other, because the more Awareness and Acceptance you develop, the more Alternatives you will consider and the more Action you will want to take.

Sheila's Approach

> *Whenever I work with a client who is depressed, frustrated, or just generally stuck, I begin by helping them identify their strengths—the inner resources that helped them survive all the way up until today. Remember how difficult it was for Cindy, living with a depressed mother who couldn't take care of her? Just think. Cindy must have some very special qualities inside of her in order to survive such neglect, lack of expressed love, and real abandonment. It was tough, but she made it. Her inner power helped her survive.*

We all have an inner force and we have to recognize it. Be **AWARE** of it. **ACCEPT** it, and then put it to use in considering **ALTERNATIVES.** While considering alternatives, ask yourself: What will I do with that force now that I recognize it is there? Examine your wants. Go for it, all the way. Bring it up and out to help you take **ACTION.**

The following are some ways of using awareness and acceptance to help you change some of your unwanted behaviors. You can use these to help you get your wants and to help you deal with BIG stuck spots:

- Identify your wants.
- What are you telling yourself that is stopping you from going after what you want, taking risks, or being assertive? What self-defeating messages hold you back?
- To what past experiences do these self-defeating messages relate? What are the messages that now "rubber-band" back to you?
- Consider 5 **Possible Positive Outcomes** (page 57) that could occur if you go after your wants.
- Identify 5 **existing strengths** that have helped you survive so far.

Example: Sheila

1. I wanted to travel to conferences out of town. My girlfriend, also a therapist, could not go with me.

2. I told myself, "I can't go alone." I gave myself self-defeating messages: I'll get lost. I'll be alone. No one will talk to me. I'll have a terrible time.

3. My old self-defeating messages said to me: You need someone to take care of you because you can't see where you are going. You can't ask for help. Don't go alone. People will think less of you if you are alone. (All exaggerated assumptions.)

4. My Possible Positive Outcomes: I'm fun to be with. No one will tie me down. I'll make new friends. I'll have a great time. I'll be proud of myself. I'll be able to go alone next time. I'll ask for help if I need it, and everything will be okay.

5. Existing strengths: determination, risk-taker, outgoing, makes friends easily.

Example: Bonnie

1. I want to say no more often, not do everything for everyone else. I want more time for myself.

2. Self-defeating messages: If I say no, I will lose my friends. They will think badly of me.

3. My old self-defeating messages: I have to be good and please everyone so they will like me. Others' needs are more important than mine.

4. Possible Positive Outcomes for me: more time for myself. I can please myself first some of the time. I can do things I enjoy, feel more relaxed, and more personally satisfied. My

friends and family can manage without me doing everything for them.

5. My existing strengths: hard working, coura-geous, funny, intelligent.

When you have considered the above, you have covered the **Awareness** and **Acceptance** process of the Womanpower Boosting Cycle.

Next come **Alternatives** and **Action.** Consider how Bonnie can learn to say NO:

1. Take a class in assertiveness training.

2. Take a class in self-esteem building.

3. Practice saying NO in non-threatening situa-tions.

4. Work through old self-defeating messages during psychotherapy.

Bonnie is now able to say NO, and she feels great. This has also helped her become more assertive in many other areas as well. She is confident and com-fortable with herself. She has given up having affairs for sexual satisfaction. Her marriage has become stable.

EXERCISE: REINFORCING YOUR BASKET OF BOOSTERS

Now it's time to reach for your Basket of Boosters begun in the last chapter and pile it high! Complete the following statements with a minimum of five endings for each:

Risks I have successfully taken:

Accomplishments I am proud of:

Wants I have achieved:

How I feel after completing the above:

Review your statements. This exercise should put
you in touch with Alternatives and Actions available
to you. Be proud of your successes. Feel powerful
because of the risks you have taken and desires you
have achieved. Now, think about your wants and the
amount of energy you are currently putting toward
your goals.

Awareness

Awareness is understanding what you are doing,
why, where, and how. By starting to identify your
"stuck spots," you have started moving toward awareness.

Think of the Awareness process as taking a picture
of yourself. You are standing, looking at yourself in
action. Look for what you like, what you don't like,
what you can change, and what you can't. What
makes you angry? What are you afraid of? What do
you want for yourself that you won't let yourself have?
Why do you stand in the way of getting it? What are
your squashers? What are your self-defeating messages from your past?

Become Aware of Your Own Coping Mechanisms

Coping refers to how people deal with everyday as
well as crisis situations, some of which may range
from mild to very stressful. Coping refers to the
psychological as well as practical solutions that individuals find for all of life's constantly changing situations. Each person develops coping mechanisms to
deal with the ups and downs of life. Some coping

mechanisms are good and helpful, while others may be ineffective and even hurtful.

Coping mechanisms, also known as *defense mechanisms,* are behaviors we adapt to protect ourselves from pain, hurt, and anxiety. They can be useful or destructive. Such mechanisms may include being a "good girl" to hide fear of rejection, building walls around us as a protective device, turning off feelings, turning to "quick-fixes" such as food, drugs, alcohol, spending money, or promiscuous sexual activity. For adult women, these patterns become destructive and are not helpful to boosting self-esteem. Sometimes women develop phobias, obsessive–compulsive behaviors, and aggressiveness as protective defenses against fears and anxieties.

If you have suffered and have developed coping mechanisms as a result, you may be stronger in the long run. If you feel powerless and have a low sense of self-esteem, identify its source. Let the source become powerful, and use the power.

Remember Bonnie The Butterfly, who was sent to her grandma's with warnings: "Be quiet. Don't get Grandma upset."? She was the perfect "good girl." As a child this may have worked well, but as an adult, it is an unhealthy coping mechanism. Always being quiet and "good" and staying out of trouble was frustrating and unsatisfying for her.

Dolly's and Rhonda's Awareness

Meet Dolly. She developed her defense mechanisms nisms when she was 8 years old. Her father drank, and after an alcoholic binge, became physically and verbally abusive to her mother. She feared that he might hurt her, too, so she often hid under the dining-room table during violent arguments. Finally her father left her and her mother. As a child, she came to some conclusions: Men yell after they have been drinking. Men are mean to their wives. Men cannot be trusted. They can hurt you and will leave you when you need them.

As an adult, Dolly became fearful of a long-term, committed relationship. Whenever a man wanted to get serious, live with her, or get married, Dolly put up her protective shield. In her mind, she associated commitment with pain, abuse, and abandonment. She feared that she was unlovable and that any man who could love her would abuse her and leave. "I'll leave them before they leave me" was her attitude.

Becoming aware of how the past affected her present, Dolly realized that although it was true that her father was abusive and caused emotional pain, not all men were abusive. Some are loving, kind, and will stay in a loving, committed relationship. Dolly needs to begin tearing down her own cocoon and allow a close relationship with a man to develop slowly.

After you understand your own coping mechanisms and your own squashers, you will learn in the Alternatives step how to make positive affirmations to replace your squashers.

Achieving self-awareness isn't easy because often it is hard to see your own behaviors. Behaviors are automatic, involuntary, and habitual reactions. Awareness is bringing those automatic responses from your unconscious self to your conscious self. Awareness means changing habitual responses to conscious, planned alternatives.

Perhaps you are like Rhonda. She stays stuck in her clerical job instead of going into sales because she is afraid to speak in front of people. You'll learn to look at yourself in new ways, respond and react differently to what you want to change and to say "I can" instead of "No, I can't."

Rhonda became aware that her teacher back in fourth grade squashed her self-esteem when she tried to speak up in front of the class. All the kids laughed because the teacher had criticized Rhonda's plaid skirt and flowered blouse combination. The teacher said, "How can your mother let you dress like that!"

Rhonda, ashamed, vowed she would never humiliate herself by getting up in front of people. And, later in high school, there were several occasions when Rhonda had to recite before classes. Remembering the earlier criticism, she worked hard at her appearance but always felt that she didn't quite measure up to everyone else and was inadequate.

That was the old Rhonda; the new Rhonda wants to move up in the company and be seen and heard. "Not everyone is like my fourth-grade teacher," she says.

Or are you like Dolly and feel that you just aren't lovable and there are no men you can trust? You may have tried and tried, but are fearful of a committed, intimate relationship. With awareness, Dolly thought about her childhood and how her alcoholic father paid too little attention to her and abused her mother. He was drunk much of the time and verbally abusive. Her mother was passive and afraid of her father. Dolly and her mother tried to please him and not upset him. Because of the way her father treated her mother, Dolly felt distant from her father and close to her mother. Dolly grew up with the squasher: "It's okay to have close relationships with women because they are loving and you can count on them. It's not okay to trust men because they are unreliable and can really hurt you."

Think about the squashers you give yourself. Where did they come from? If they are from childhood, from a parent, teacher, or because of an event that happened long ago, put things into perspective. Link the origins of these messages to your own squashers. What you once believed was true may not be true for you now. Don't routinely base your future expectations on your past experiences. Just because your mother may have told you "Don't go near the water. You'll fall in" doesn't mean that you can't take a cruise and have a good time. Learn to enjoy yourself! Just because Dolly's father didn't pay enough atten-

tion to her as she was growing up, doesn't mean that
all men in her life will treat her abusively. What was
real for her then, doesn't have to be real for her now.
Once Dolly became aware of this truth, she was ready
to move on to the next step: Acceptance. You can do
it, too.

Acceptance

Acceptance is acknowledging the truth of what you
become aware of and taking responsibility for what
you are and the way you act. In Bonnie's case, she
became aware that while she blamed her husband for
her own passivity, she allowed it. "I sacrificed myself.
I never said no, even when I wanted to. It was my
responsibility to make choices."

In Rhonda's case, she may have thought, "Everyone
else gets promoted before me. They won't let me get
ahead." The truth is that she never asked for a
promotion into sales because she was afraid of standing up to speak in front of meetings. Now she is aware
that **she** is responsible for her lack of promotion. The
truth is that she had actually turned down two promotions in the last two years. Today she accepts the fact
that changing her situation is in her power.

The *opposite* of acceptance is *resisting acceptance.*
Without acceptance, some women may blame others
for their lack of promotion, going from job to job
without real satisfaction, or saying that men get all the
lucky breaks, rather than realizing that they themselves contribute to their own situations.

With an understanding of acceptance, learn to
change your behavior from automatic, habitual, to
conscious and constructive, and learn to take responsibility for your behavior choices and the feelings that
go with these choices.

Men and Women: Are Power Differences Real?

Many women let themselves be intimidated by powerful people and fear speaking up. In the Awareness step, the passive, non-assertive woman begins to realize that because of her low self-esteem, she has allowed men *and* women to dominate her. Because of her attitudes and behaviors, she has given her power away. With awareness, she begins to realize that she is in control of her power. With acceptance, she feels her power, takes responsibility for herself and her treatment by others. At this point you are ready to start thinking about Alternatives.

Alternatives

This step means paying more attention to your personal boosters rather than your squashers. Alternatives mean allowing your boosters to work for you in making more productive choices. Previously, your squashers were in your way; now it's time to look beyond them.

What are your strengths? Recognize and acknowledge your power. Realize that you have choices and options for your behavior and feelings. Explore your choices.

Look at the following list of your PERSONAL RIGHTS.

PERSONAL RIGHTS

Giving yourself permission for:

Freedom
Choice
Options
Risk
Action

Power
Self-esteem

Ask yourself the following:

- What are ten of your existing strengths? (Think of even more if you can.)
- How have these strengths helped you survive?
- a) accomplish your goals so far?
- b) overcome your obstacles?
- What new behaviors and actions would you like to take?
- Look back at your list of "I wants." Which of your strengths will counteract the squashers that block action?

How Dolly Used Alternatives

Dolly allowed her fear of losing love to be so overwhelming that she blocked any intimacy with kind and loving men. In learning about alternatives, she discovered that many men who are loving and kind will stay. She realized that she deserves to feel good about herself, her life, and her relationships. She realized that she is the one who blocks her way toward a close relationship.

After a few months in therapy, Dolly joined a self-esteem class, enrolled in a workshop on self-esteem and intimacy, and joined a women's support group. Now she is in a satisfying relationship with a new man. She feels lovable and loved.

Possible Positive Outcomes

Part of the Alternatives step is considering Possible *Positive* Outcomes that might result if you changed your behavior or thought about yourself in different ways. Like Dolly, what do you think might happen if you began to trust a man who said he loved you?

Part of the concept of Alternatives includes learning to use an important technique: **guided imagery or visualization**—the process through which you can visualize yourself in your new experience or place, taking risks, or making changes.

⬛⬛⬛⬛⬛⬛⬛⬛⬛⬛⬛⬛⬛⬛⬛⬛⬛⬛⬛⬛⬛⬛

EXERCISE: A VISUALIZATION TECHNIQUE

Here's a guided imagery exercise I have used with thousands of women in various groups:

Close your eyes. Relax yourself by slowing down your breathing. Say over and over again to yourself: "Body calm. Body relax." Then bring in an image that relaxes you, for example, white light or a slow, rolling ocean wave. The white light feels warm and healing. Allow the white light to relax and heal you more. Then see yourself as the person you want to be. Feel your sense of accomplishment, success, and satisfaction. Feel empowered.

Guided imagery is powerful because it helps you see and experience yourself in the new behavior. You can make an audiotape for yourself or buy one. Use the tape to help you make affirmations that will help you visualize positive pictures. With visualization, you can boost self-esteem related to physical, emotional, or behavioral symptoms.

⬛⬛⬛⬛⬛⬛⬛⬛⬛⬛⬛⬛⬛⬛⬛⬛⬛⬛⬛⬛⬛⬛

PERSONAL WORKBOOK

Title a page:
MY GOODIE BASKET OF PLEASURES
When you have taken a positive step toward Womanpower and are feeling proud of yourself, give yourself

a reward. Make your own personal "goodie basket" and select rewards for yourself occasionally.

Here's how: Make a list of things you enjoy. For each success, reward yourself with choices from your basket. Each woman's satisfactions differ. Think what would really please you. For a change, put yourself first. Indulge.

Here are a few suggestions for treats and self-indulgences:

- Get a video you want to see
- Get a book you want to read from the library
- Buy a new hat
- Spend an hour in an outdoor garden or an indoor conservatory
- Take a bubble bath without regard for time
- If you're near a beach in the summer, take a walk along the water
- Get a massage, manicure, pedicure or facial
- Have lunch at a favorite restaurant with a special friend
- Make a long distance call to an old friend
- Take time to write a letter
- Spend an afternoon at your favorite museum
- Take a walk through an interesting neighborhood
- Get tickets to a popular play
- Go shopping; buy some "fun clothes"
- Spend a day doing what you like to do best

What Do You Fear Most?

As part of the Alternatives step, you can develop your own personal risk hierarchy. Work on overcoming the easy ones first so you can build confidence in yourself. Confidence will help you conquer the harder tasks.

PERSONAL WORKBOOK

Title a page:
MY PERSONAL RISK HIERARCHY

Rank the things you fear risking most at the top of the page and minor fears at the bottom. For example: (Higher anxiety at top. Lower anxiety level at bottom of page with lowest number.)

10 Telling my husband I'll leave him because he is abusive to me

9 Discussing separation with my husband

8 Going on a new job search

7 Figuring out how to make more money so I can be self-supporting

6 Going back to school

5 Applying for my own credit cards

4 Joining a support group

3 Attending Alanon

2 Signing up for a self-esteem class

1 Going to a lecture on self-esteem

Each accomplishment builds confidence and courage to go for the next step.

General Power Boosters That Work for Many Women

Some women receive boosters from nurturing parents who say, "You CAN do it." Some women receive boosters from role models. Then there are some general boosters that can help you pull out what was always within yourself. All boosters empower you to support, encourage, and give approval and praise to yourself. Here are some examples of general power boosters:

Things will work out.
I can learn how.
I learn quickly.
I am smart.
I am creative.
I am capable.
I am likable and lovable.
I am fun to be with.
I can have a good time.
My feelings and opinions count.
I deserve respect.
I can say NO sometimes.

Make New Decisions

Based on consideration of your Possible Positive Outcomes, you can now make some new decisions about yourself. Write a memo to yourself. Tell a friend about your new decisions. Writing or telling will help reinforce it in your own mind.

Sometimes it is helpful to go back into the past to understand your current reactions. For some individuals this can be difficult to do alone; psychotherapy with the right therapist can help with personal decision work.

Learn to Make Affirmations (Internal Self-Boosters)

During the Alternatives step, learn to make affirmations about your internal power boosters—positive self-talk in action form. For example, say to yourself:

- I can tackle this.
- I can figure this out.
- I am lovable.
- I am competent
- I will be successful.

Learn to phrase your own affirmations. Here's the formula:

I will use my (strengths) to get what I want (goal) so that I can (Possible Positive Outcome).

I will use my determination and will power to lose 25 pounds in order to feel proud of my body and fit into my smaller clothes.

Make affirmations for each of your previously listed wants. As demonstrated above, take one, two, or three of your strengths and start on your Affirmation process with the strength, then at least two Possible Positive Outcomes. Now you're ready for action!

Action

Use your energy to take action—putting into practice all that you have learned about yourself during your work on Awareness, Acceptance, and Alternatives. This is the time to gather your courage. Try something new. Take one small step at a time. Small steps will make it easier. After each step, enjoy your rewards. Share your results with a friend or write them down.

Begin your Action step by setting some long- and short-term goals, taking risks, doing what you want, and having a healthier perception of yourself. Taking action means making personal decisions, entering the unknown and the unfamiliar, stepping out of your "comfort zone." At first you may feel scared and nervous, but once you take each new step, you'll find that it gets easier. If you write down your progress steps, you will have something to look back on.

It may be a little frightening when you move away from your familiar responses to unknown areas of action, but you'll be excited by the possibilities of good things happening for you.

Refer back to the page in your Personal Workbook: RISK HIERARCHY. Choose the lowest step on your risk hierarchy and work on it. Once you have been successful with the least anxiety-producing risk, you will feel encouraged to go on.

When considering taking action toward developing more Womanpower, think in terms of "staying safe and stuck" vs. "taking risks and moving forward." By taking risks and realizing possible advantages you will let yourself promote personal growth, personal well-being and personal power.

Rhonda's Risk

I feared speaking in front of a group and decided to take a risk. I decided to speak at the church breakfast group just to try my capability before asking for a job promotion that involved speaking at sales meetings. I began my talk at the church breakfast by telling the audience that I was scared of standing in front of them. My face turned red. I told the audience that I was nervous. As soon as I saïd it out loud, I was able to relax and knew that I would do well. Everyone loved my talk. Now I feel more confident about doing it again. Once I let go of my old fear, I was okay.

Your Risks, Your Decisions

For you, Action may mean asserting yourself to your boss, saying all the things you have wanted to tell him but have been afraid to say. It may mean leaving a bad relationship because you have been unhappy but afraid to leave because you think no one else would want you.

For Dolly, it meant taking a chance on trusting a man. For Rhonda, it meant gathering confidence by speaking in front of her church group. She's had several other successes, and now she's ready to think seriously about taking the next job promotion that involves public speaking.

Recognize that your own personal truth is a strength. It makes you more real and human.

Action Requires a Plan

Just as you make a shopping list before going to the supermarket, part of your Action step involves making a plan. Think about your long-term and short-term goals—your short-term goals will help you get to your long-term goals.

❋❋❋❋❋❋❋❋❋❋❋❋❋❋❋❋❋❋❋

PERSONAL WORKBOOK

Title a page:
MY PERSONAL ACTION PLAN
List your long-term goals, wants, dreams. For example: Lose 25 pounds

Get out of an unhealthy relationship

Meet another man who is more likely to meet my needs

Go out to more social activities

Feel attractive and learn to flirt

Build my self-esteem

List your short-term goals that will help you reach long-term goals above. For example, for wanting to lose 25 pounds, start with short-term steps:

1) Sign up for an aerobics class; get into an exercise routine
2) Firm up my body
3) Change my eating habits; no more junk food
4) Reduce my overall food intake

5) Fill my life with other enjoyable activities to replace my need for fatty food

EXERCISE: MAKE A CONTRACT WITH YOURSELF

For each of your goals in your Personal Action Plan, take one page and state that goal. List the reasons you want to achieve this. Then list the steps you will take to make certain this happens. Write down the reward you will give yourself when you achieve your goal. Now date and sign the page.

Now put these pages at the back of your personal workbook.

Review the Four "A" Steps of the Womanpower Boosting Cycle

Here's a quick summary of the Womanpower Boosting Cycle. Continue to apply the steps as you read through the following chapters.

Awareness

Consider the following:

- Describe a desire, risk, or change you are currently holding yourself back from realizing.
- What squashers hold you back from feeling good about your life or being successful? What specific squashers keep you from going after what you want?
- How are your squashers related to your past? Where did they come from? What are your self-defeating messages? Why are they in your head?

- What's your new awareness? How does it relate to past experience? How does it relate to your current beliefs which influence your action and reaction?
- Review the page in your Personal Workbook that you began at the beginning of this chapter (page 65).

Acceptance

- What responsibilities do you now claim as your own?
- What behaviors do you acknowledge that contribute to your stuck-spot scores?
- What changes have you made in your attitudes and outlooks?
- Review all Personal Workbook pages.

Alternatives

- What other choices and new boosters will you act upon?
- What Possible Positive Outcomes have you considered?
- Name five Possible Positive Outcomes that could happen if you go after your dreams.
- Which of your strengths help you deal with life?

Action

- What will you do to get going?
- Make a contract with yourself.

When you've answered these questions and talked with yourself about each of the four "A" steps, you've worked through the Womanpower Boosting process. However, you will want to return many times to each step.

Move Toward Womanpower: Use Your Best Wheels

The four "A" steps of the Womanpower Boosting Cycle are an ongoing, lifelong process. The intertwining of the steps never ends. With each risk and change, you'll have more power and more self-esteem.

The strongest wheels move you forward and can help you get unstuck. The Wheel of Growth, which follows, is positive-energy charging and will help you.

WHEEL OF GROWTH

Now make your own Wheel of Boosters, based on your alternatives and the action plans you intend to take. Add another page to your Personal Workbook, patterned after this Wheel.

The following is the Wheel of Defeat, which is energy-draining. It emphasizes your STUCK SPOTS (which you now know how to overcome).

WHEEL OF DEFEAT

Draw your own Wheel of Defeat, based on things you now understand about yourself. It is understandable that you may feel frustrated and angry just thinking about your own self-defeating messages. Now is the time! Change the energy from your anger into positive energy. Push your Wheel of Defeat to the back of your life. It will only hold you back if you don't push it back first.

After you have drawn up your Wheel of Defeat, take the page and squash it between your hands. Crunch it. Feel the powerful action of destroying it. Throw it into the garbage can. Be proud that you have thrown away your negative-energy draining force. Good for you!

Now reach into your Goodie Basket of Pleasures (page 80) and select a reward for yourself. Indulge yourself. You deserve it. You've done a good job!

In the next chapter you will learn more about Womanpower—how to become more assertive and use assertiveness as another Womanpower tool!

4

TAKE THE NEXT STEP:
ASSERT YOURSELF

Are you tired of being manipulated? Do you say what you feel, express your beliefs and opinions, stand up for your rights? Can you say NO and stick to it?

In the preceding chapters you learned how to apply the concepts of boosters, squashers, self-defeating messages and the four "A" steps of behavior change toward achieving Womanpower: *Awareness, Acceptance, Alternatives, and Action.* Now you are ready to take another step to improve your self-esteem in your personal, social, school, and work relationships. This additional step is *assertiveness,* which you can use to help the other steps work even more effectively.

In this chapter, you will learn more about how to think and react assertively, believe in yourself, value what you have to say, stand up for what you believe, know that you have the right of personal choice and that you accept the responsibility and consequences of your own choices. You will learn to feel good about yourself, your feelings, thoughts, opinions, and needs, and then feel good about expressing them. You will learn to stop letting people walk all over you, manipulate you, or take advantage of you. You will learn to understand differences between:

- Non-assertiveness
- Assertiveness
- Aggressiveness

Why Are Many Women Non-Assertive?

We all know women who behave passively and live their lives in subservience to everyone else. They are the smilers, caretakers, and doers for everyone else. They were told: "Be nice. Be a good girl. Don't rock the boat." Generations of young women grew up hearing these messages. Some women accepted these positions because they may have had less education, felt economically dependent, were afraid of being alone, or may have been told "you're only a pretty face." Many felt insecure. Many felt no sense of self.

For many women, insecure feelings result in:
A) holding back: being nice or good in order to get positive reactions, not expressing feelings or thoughts, non-assertive behavior, or saying what they think others want to hear.

or

B) becoming tough (the "bitch") and aggressive, by putting others down.

Non-assertive women feel powerless. They see others as more important or better than they are; they seek approval from others. They hold back their real feelings. Everything they do is geared to pleasing others. They deny their own lovability. They don't value themselves.

Non-assertive women often speak apologetically. How often do you hear, "You're going to think what I have to say is dumb . . ." or "I'm sorry to have to tell you this . . ." or "I know you'll get mad when you hear this . . ." With statements like these, women are discounting what they have to say. Non-assertive women use "hedging" language. They beat around the bush. For example, one might say, "The garbage is full." What she really means is, "I'd like you to please take out the garbage." Remember that we don't have glass heads, so others cannot see inside to know what we want unless we ask.

Frequently using phrases like "you know" and "I mean" is a sign of being unsure, looking for approval, recognition, or acknowledgment. Some women fear confrontation and conflict. At some time in their lives they learned "peace at any price." Maybe Mom gave in a lot to avoid arguing with a loud, noisy, or abusive Dad, or vice-versa. Maybe Dad kept quiet to avoid the overly aggressive Mom. In either case, there was no good role modeling for communication or fair fighting.

Examples of Some Non-Assertive Women

Susan

> *My mother was very aggressive and domineering. I learned to stay out of the way to avoid her tirades. As I grew up, I became afraid of mean people. I tried to be invisible at work. I got passed over for promotions. The internal squashing message I hear is "a small defenseless girl just stays out of the way. If people notice me they might hurt me."*

Nancy

> *When I saw my father hitting my mother, I would hit him back. I became a female bully. "No one messes with me," was the message I later gave my schoolmates. Underneath I was scared, depressed, and lonely. The truth is that I was petrified to let my guard down because I know that men can hurt.*

As a result, Nancy goes from aggressively acting out her anger to a fear reaction, non-assertiveness, and holding back her real reaction, which is fear of being hurt. To herself she says: "I'll get you before you get me," and "I'm afraid to let you get too close because you might hurt me."

Natalie

Natalie is five feet tall, and a highly professional woman. She always wears very high heels, even though they are uncomfortable.

> *I became aggressive and tough, because I believed that I would increase my credibility and power that way. Because I am so small, I felt that men, especially, would not take me seriously or respect me in the business world.*

Natalie's "Napoleon" complex makes her personally unlikeable. It is hard to be with her because she is either defensive or on the offense and ready for a fight. She is pushing away just what she is looking for— acceptance.

Non-Assertiveness and Codependency

Codependent women feel powerless and are usually non-assertive because they are not true to themselves. They deceive themselves and cover up their own real feelings. Many feel like victims, stuck, and immobilized. Codependent women don't risk confrontation—they think the price is too high. They allow themselves to stay in the background of another person's life. They set up this situation because they are afraid. They do not realize they have alternatives, choices, and options regarding their actions. Here's Barbara:

> *My husband used a lot of marijuana and sometimes other drugs. I was depressed because I was fat and passive. I was scared, felt powerless, and*

thought my feelings were not important. Even though at times he was abusive, I couldn't leave him because I thought no one else would want me.

After going through the Womanpower Boosting Cycle, Barbara realized that her feelings *are* important and *do* matter. She let her husband know how angry she was with him and that she wasn't going to let him abuse her anymore. Today she feels lighter and has a sense of power and freedom that she never felt before. She went on a diet and lost ten pounds within the first two weeks. She is determined to lose more weight and thus continue to empower herself.

You'll read more about codependency and other relationships in Chapter 6.

Non-assertive and *aggressive* behaviors are both very unhealthy, ineffective, and non-productive. We will describe these behaviors and then show you a model for effective assertiveness to use at home, school, or work. Once you learn how to be assertive, you will feel your power and then be able to express what you have to say and what you want, rather than suppress or repress, deny or avoid, or defer your thoughts or feelings. You will realize that what you have to say is just as important as the next person, male or female. No one else's thoughts or feelings are better or more important than yours.

You may recognize some familiar threads from stories told by other women.

Jenny

As the youngest of four girls, I felt ignored. So I decided to be perfect, please everyone, and do what everyone wanted me to do so they would love and accept me. I held back what I really felt and never asked for anything for myself. In my marriage and at work, I did the same thing. As a result, I got extremely depressed and had frequent headaches. When I became aware that my passivity and non-assertiveness were hurting me, I realized that I had a choice to be assertive. I started to feel better about myself.

Caroline:

I was the child who arrived fifteen years after my older sister. My older sister took care of me a lot of the time. Sometimes my parents hardly acknowledged that I was there. So I became extra good, nice, and tried to please, hoping to get noticed and loved. When I got married, I hoped my husband would be nice to me. What I didn't realize before we were married was that he was a narcissistic person, very self-centered. I thought that if I "fed" his ego, he would like me better. I wound up acting completely non-assertive with him. I was always deferring to him as though he was the most important person in this relationship.

After twenty-five years of giving in I decided I couldn't give up any more of myself by allowing him to control me. I had to separate, be me, think for myself and do some of my own things. When I told my husband this, he panicked, got insecure and scared because I would no longer feed his narcissistic ego. I found out that his controlling self came from his own deep feelings of fear and insecurity. When I assert myself, he cries and acts out like a child.

What an awareness-breakthrough for me! All this time, I had been scared of him and afraid to assert myself. The truth is that, of the two of us, I'm more powerful, and he is really weaker. Now we're separated, a divorce is pending, and he has to fend for himself. His problems are no longer my problems.

In both examples, neither Jenny or Caroline really got the approval they hoped for by being non-assertive. Instead they continued to be stepped on and ignored, and they never really felt loved or accepted. Actually, they set up the feelings of low self-worth that they were trying to avoid without knowing it. Within a few months of becoming aware of the real truths, Caroline started taking positive steps.

The myth: If you are nice and please everyone, they will love you and give you what you want.

The truth: If you continue pleasing others, you will feel unloved because you don't love yourself. People will treat you like a doormat.

There is no possible payoff in being or thinking non-assertively. With assertiveness training, you can learn to see through others' insecurities. Many women need to realize that we do not have to allow aggressors to push us around, demean, or manipulate us. It is our choice how we spend our time and how we lead our lives. In the examples above, the realization that Jenny and Caroline actually had power—that they really were stronger than their weak husbands who were using aggressive behavior as a cover up—was a real insight. Both women soon began to feel their power and started to assert themselves.

Non-Assertiveness vs. Assertiveness

Non-assertiveness is the opposite of assertiveness. A non-assertive woman holds back her feelings; she doesn't let herself feel good about what she does or has to say. She gives the impression that she is not important. Others are more important. The rights of others are more important than hers. The non-assertive woman acts out on these beliefs. She actually gives away her rights and keeps hardly anything for herself. This frustrates her with feelings of powerlessness and helplessness, and makes her vulnerable.

Non-assertiveness is being stuck in the cocoon, feeling walled in, closed in, hiding behind your self-created walls and not seeing your way out. You are your own judge, jury, and prosecutor. You are the keeper of the key to prison or freedom.

Non-Assertiveness Means that You:

- hold back, avoid, deny, suppress, or defer to others, not feeling that what you have to say is important, or worth saying.
- let others walk all over you, not realizing that you have the right to do something about it.
- feel frustrated and badly about yourself and get angry when you don't stand up for yourself. You feel like a doormat and permit people to wipe their feet all over you!
- project a weak image, denying and being afraid of hurting others.
- make it hard for others to get to know you.

Holding back your feelings causes anxiety and inner tension to build up. When a non-assertive woman fills up with enough anger and rage, she may erupt like a volcano externally and become aggressive or implode internally. Neither reaction is healthy. It is hard for others to get to know you because they have no way of knowing what you are really thinking or feeling if you don't say what's on your mind. We expect people to read our minds, and when they don't, we feel resentful.

Move Toward Assertiveness

Assertiveness is important in all aspects of daily life, from your most personal relationships to those in business. Assertiveness is communication with other people in a direct, honest manner. It's saying what's on your mind: *I think, I feel, I need.* It is being able to express four basic feelings of *sadness, anger, happiness* or *fear.* It is saying what you mean and meaning what you say.

With assertiveness, you recognize that you have the right to stand up for yourself—your actions, feelings, opinions, and needs—and that you must respect the same in others. It is give and take. It is saying, ***"I am important and so are you. I have respect for me and for you. We are equal."***

Assertiveness helps you feel good about yourself. It's putting your own internal force into action to resist being dominated or manipulated by others. Assertive women ask for what they want. They take risks. Assertive women speak out and go forward. They see Possible Positive Outcomes. They have a better chance of achieving their goals. Assertive women have self-confidence and self-esteem. You can have it, too.

Assertiveness Means that You:

- let others know what is going on with you, whether it is what you feel, think, want, or need, and that you accept responsibility for what you say and do.
- project equality in your dealings with others.
- feel self-respect and proud of yourself.
- accept human error as a part of life.
- realize that not everyone in the world will like or love you.
- realize that you are the most important person you know.

Assertiveness is knowing that you can let yourself out of your self-made cocoon. It is the key to realizing your own worth as a person and feeling your power—

and flying free like a butterfly, landing where you choose.

Assertiveness can make you a more active participant in your life. It can give you a chance to get more of what you want. For example, in a love relationship or in a work situation, it is easier to have a close and satisfying relationship with a person who is assertive because you know where they stand. Assertive people are straightforward, direct, and open, which makes closeness easier when desired and more effective with any relationship.

ASSERTIVENESS: HOW DO YOU RATE YOURSELF?

In the following scale, rate yourself from 1–10 on each question, with 1 being low and 10 being high. For example: "I let others tell me what to do." If you never let others boss you around, give yourself a 10. If you let others tell you what to do about half the time, give yourself a 5.

ASSERTIVENESS SELF-RATING SCALE

1. I often have a hard time saying NO. _____
2. I let people often take advantage of me. _____
3. I hesitate to express my opinion. _____
4. I often don't know what to say to attractive persons of the opposite sex. _____
5. I hesitate to make or accept dates because I am scared. _____
6. I avoid confronting other people when they hurt me. _____
7. If a close and respected relative is annoying me, I smother my feelings rather than express my annoyance. _____

8. I avoid asking questions for fear of saying something stupid. _____

9. I usually avoid an argument by swallowing and giving in. _____

10. During an argument, I am afraid that I will get so upset, I will shake all over. _____

11. When I have done something important or worthwhile, I manage to hide it from others so I won't feel embarrassed. _____

12. When the food served at a restaurant is not done to my satisfaction, I will not send it back. I'll either just eat it or leave it. _____

13. If a salesperson has gone to considerable trouble to show me merchandise that is not quite suitable, I have a difficult time saying NO. _____

14. I often avoid returning merchandise because I am afraid and embarrassed. _____

15. I avoid arguing over prices with clerks and salespeople. _____

If you found yourself answering more than from five to eight of the above questions with a low number, let the examples of other women you read about in this chapter help you. Consider your own personal strengths; build upon them.

Getting Results with Assertiveness

Bernice was a "pleaser" personality type, and usually didn't want to stir up any trouble. But she got to a point where she felt overworked and overwhelmed. She made a decision to become assertive and talk to her boss. She had been at her job for two years and then was promoted to supervisor. But due to cutbacks, she wasn't replaced for her desk duties, so she really did two jobs, often staying late without overtime pay. She couldn't handle the situation any longer. She got headaches, sometimes had to take days off, and was making more and more mistakes. Her body told her she had to do something. So she went to her boss.

How Bernice Used Assertiveness

Bernice:
"I appreciate the promotion you gave me. I enjoy supervising my staff. I want you to know that I am not dissatisfied, but you've probably noticed that I've been absent a lot lately, and I'm sick and starting to make mistakes. I've tried to do it all, but I just can't."
(She has defined the situation, states her position, and says what's going on.)
"I can't do it all. I need help, either a part- or full-time assistant."
(She acknowledges the situation and then makes an assertive statement.)

Boss:
"I'm glad you told me. I didn't know. I did notice your absences. But money is tight. We can't hire another person."
(Boss acknowledges Bernice's viewpoint and gives feedback.)

Bernice:
"Do you have any ideas? I know money is tight."
(Bernice indicates that she is open to compromise.)

Boss:
"Maybe we can hire a temp once a week; I think we can budget a day a week. And you can start delegating some work. I'll call a meeting."
(Bernice hears the options. She feels good, even though she isn't getting all of what she wants.)

Bernice:
"How soon?"
(Bernice takes action.)

Bernice has presented her wants. She also respects her boss's feelings. Before using her assertiveness, Bernice was carrying excessive baggage that got in the way of her productivity. Once she faced up to her boss, she felt freed up, both physically and emotionally.

Once you recognize a problem as excess baggage, as Bernice did, say to yourself: "I'm no longer going to carry this problem." Don't let it weigh you down. Deal with it as close to the time of the difficult situation as possible so it won't intrude on your productivity, your action, and your self-esteem.

How Is Assertiveness Different from AGGRESSIVENESS

Many women, in their effort to become more assertive, become more like what they perceive some men to be. They bypass *assertiveness* and move into *aggressive behavior*. People who behave aggressively look for attention by expressing their anger and frustration in negative ways, such as sarcasm, temper tantrums, and rebelliousness.

To the world, the aggressive person shouts, "I'm OK. I know everything. Don't tell me what to do." For many, this is all a cover-up. Many who have been hurt in the past adopt this "bully" stance (tough on the outside, but scared and insecure underneath).

Aggressors act out their anger and pick fights with those they perceive as weaker. Aggressors seek out non-assertors because they can take power *from* them. Aggressors get power at the expense of others. Aggressive women really do not have high self-esteem. They appear loud and tough but are really unhappy and discontent inside.

Sheila's Turning Point:
Assertiveness with My Superior

Long before I became a therapist, I once had a boss who was an aggressive businesswoman. One of her legs was shorter and thinner than the other from childhood polio. As a child, kids picked on her and called her names, and she hated it. Kids can either decide to fight or flee when this happens. Bobbe decided to fight. She became a little bully and became tough and mean.

As an adult, she did the same thing. She put everyone down, including me. She was demeaning and used abusive language. She only gave criticism, never support. She was very controlling and really turned everyone off. No one trusted her. She was extremely unproductive and unmotivating.

After a while on the job, I was afraid of her and felt powerless. She often humiliated me. A major turning point in my life came when I read a book on assertiveness. I joined a personal-growth class and had psychological counseling. From what I learned, I decided to tell my boss what I felt about her constant criticism and humiliation.

One day I said to her, "I don't mind that you tell me what I do wrong, but there is no reason to treat me in this demeaning way."

She reacted, "Why didn't you tell me this before. I didn't know you were so sensitive. I thought you could handle it."

I said, "Now you know, I am sensitive." I felt such relief in having said this that I started to cry. I then left her office to compose myself.

Later in the day she said, "I have to apologize. I value you tremendously."

I came to realize that I had allowed this woman to bully me, and she was more scared of life than I am. If I'm feeling this way, there must be millions of women like me.

Usually aggressors push everyone away. They don't want anyone to get too close, because they do not want to be hurt or seen through. They control, manipulate, and threaten to hurt. The aggressive behavior is really a cover-up for fear, insecurity, and real powerlessness.

Aggressiveness Means that You:

- get your point across, but don't care who you hurt, discount, or demean while doing it.
- try to put yourself above others by putting them down, which is really false power.
- stand up for your rights at the expense of other people.
- put other people down to build yourself up.
- blame others for mistakes and not take responsibility. "I get my rights by denying yours."
- feed off of non-assertive people.
- feel loaded with hurt and anger which you dump onto others.
- feel scared to release control.

Sometime an aggressive woman, especially in business, thinks to herself: "I'm this way because I'm afraid you're not going to believe me if I act too nice." She believes that she has to be loud and mean to be heard or to make her point, especially with powerful men. She is flippant, sarcastic and demeaning. Aggressors get their power by demeaning other people.

ARE YOU AGGRESSIVE?

If you are aggressive, you will probably answer YES to most of the following questions:

ARE YOU AGGRESSIVE?

	YES	NO
Do you enjoy controlling others?		
Are you rigid and inflexible?		
Do you put others down to build yourself up?		
Do you always have to be right?		
Do you have difficulty admitting to mistakes?		
Do you hide your real feelings, especially fear?		
Do you show superiority to others?		
Are your sometimes sarcastic?		
Do you use demeaning language?		
Are you often defensive?		
Do you enjoy being with others who you feel are inferior?		
Do you intimidate others to get what you want?		
Were you ever described as a bitch or a bully?		

If you think you are too aggressive, think about how you would turn the statements above around to reflect assertive behavior.

Passive Aggression

Another form of manipulation is known as *passive aggression* or *indirect aggression,* which is manipulation by guilt or shame.

Here's an example: Three women are on a car trip together. They stop in a small town; after lunch they agree to each go their separate ways for shopping and to meet at the car at three o'clock. The driver, A, has been building up anger against B and C because they were not ready to leave early in the morning at the agreed upon time. B and C return to the car as agreed, at three o'clock. A, who has the car keys, doesn't show up. The two suspect the driver of deliberately not showing up to show her power by keeping them waiting, which in fact is what the driver, A, has done. That's passive aggression. Other passive aggressive behaviors include pouting, sulking, and the silent treatment, all designed to "get" the other person.

"Compliments" can also be a form of passive aggression. Have you ever heard one friend look at another's new purchase and, rather than admire it, say "I wish I could afford that!"? Or, when meeting a friend wearing a new knockout fur coat for the first time, say, "I didn't know you had a mink coat!"

When Mary moved into a new house, she invited two friends over to see it. One friend said: "I'm so happy for you that you now have such a nice home." The other friend said: "This is much bigger than my house." Which of the friends do you think is more genuine?

Responding to Aggression

Learn to recognize aggressive behaviors in others. If you find yourself in a relationship with an aggressor, you need to develop the ability to take charge or get out. Being assertive is the best way to counteract these potentially unhealthy relationships. The assertive woman won't let the aggressor get away with his or her antics. The assertive woman will not feed or fuel the aggressor. Eventually the aggressor realizes that this behavior is not working and backs off to find someone else to abuse.

Assertiveness Requires Effective Communications

Effective communications involve both verbal and non-verbal ways of communicating with others. When both ways work well for you, you can communicate assertively and powerfully.

Verbal Communications

Verbal communications include tone of voice and choice of words. Your tone of voice can indicate a lot about you. For example, some women are whiney and their voices may sound wiggly, weak, soft, or hesitant. Whining may have helped manipulate Daddy, but it doesn't go over well in the workplace or in social situations. A woman demonstrates non-assertiveness in her choice of words. For example, she may sound apologetic. Her statements may be soft and not convincing. Her conversation is filled with "I'm sorry . . . ," "I regret . . . ," etc.

On the other hand, the assertive woman has a firm, yet soft, friendly voice, appropriate for the situation. An aggressive woman may sound tense, shrill, loud, shaky, cold, demanding, or authoritarian.

Sheila:

Once after a session of my singles support group, a woman (we'll call Janie) asked me how she could get one of the men to go out for coffee with her. I said, "You could ask him." Then I heard Janie go over to Ron and say, "You are going to think that this is so stupid, and you probably won't want to go anyway, but would you like to go out for coffee with me? Ron went anyway, despite the self-demeaning way Janie made her request!

When you apologize for what you want to ask, you reduce your credibility and the validity of your request. The words you use change the power of your message. A powerful statement would have been: "Ron, I've enjoyed talking with you during the session. I thought it would be fun to go out for coffee and continue our conversation."

Non-Assertive Phrases

The *non-assertive* person turns herself off to others by using words such as:

I'm sorry.
I regret . . .
I probably sound stupid.
I know you probably won't believe me.
I might sound foolish.

Aggressive Phrases

The AGGRESSIVE person turns herself off to others by using phrases such as:

You better . . .
You always . . .
You never . . .
What is wrong with you?
Don't you ever listen?
You should have listened.
I don't know when you will ever learn.
You don't know what you are talking about
I am so sick of you.

You can see how the aggressor feeds off the non-assertive person. Neither the non-assertive person nor the aggressive person really communicates effectively.

Non-Verbal Communications

Non-verbal communications are transmitted with body language and use of eye contact. For example, a blank stare or looking away indicates non-assertiveness. Looking away indicates shame, embarrassment, fear of exposure, or wanting to get away. A glare, looking down at or looking through another person indicates aggression. Staring may mean possible abuse, wanting to hurt or intimidate.

An assertive woman connects with another through eye contact. The woman who feels self-confident and powerful makes more eye contact and maintains it during conversation. Eye contact breeds bonding, connection, and equality. How a woman moves her body, stands, looks down at another, shakes a finger at another, demonstrates her desire for power. A woman who sits hunched over, clutching her purse in front of her, shows a scared, unapproachable, closed person. Contrast this with the open person who sits up straight, inviting another to approach. When she sits and speaks, she frequently leans toward the other, gesturing outwardly. Her body position, even while relaxed, invites friendliness and openness. Her "body language" says that she is approachable and wants others to get acquainted with her.

Assertiveness: Your Personal Rights

Everyone has personal rights. A big step toward becoming more assertive is to believe that you have them and give yourself permission to exercise them. Tell yourself that you have the right to:

Be yourself

Refuse requests without feeling selfish

Be competent and proud of your accomplishments

Feel and express anger

Ask for affection

Ask for help when you need it

Be treated as a capable adult

Make mistakes and be responsible for them

Change your mind

Some Specific Assertiveness Techniques You May Want to Try

Become Aware of Manipulation

Do you let people make you feel guilty? Guilt can stop you from doing what you want to do and makes you feel unhappy about what you have done. For example, has someone ever told you: "You don't call me. You don't love me." "If you loved me you would . . ." "After all I've done for you . . ." That's manipulation by guilt.

Guilt is like a ball thrown to you. You can choose to catch it or not to catch it. Manipulation can be direct or indirect; both kinds make you feel badly about yourself. Remember, no one can make you feel anything. You ultimately decide how you feel and behave. You can make a decision not to allow yourself to be manipulated.

Direct Confrontation with Manipulative Behavior

This is one of the best ways to handle manipulative behavior. Direct confrontation includes telling another you are affected by what they say and do. For example, you might say:

"I don't like being shouted at."

"I am uncomfortable when you shout."

"I know you're angry, but I don't feel like getting into a fight."

Be straightforward, especially with a husband, boss, family member, and co-worker. Because the risk is greater and we are afraid of rejection, it's often hardest to talk in a very straightforward manner about emotional feelings with people we love the most. You might say, "I want to tell you something, but I'm scared." To get over the scared feeling, get into it. Say it. Get through it and past it.

⬦⬦⬦⬦⬦⬦⬦⬦⬦⬦⬦⬦⬦⬦⬦⬦⬦⬦⬦

FIVE ACTION STEPS TOWARD ASSERTIVENESS AND FEELING EMPOWERED

1. Describe a situation in which you would like to be more assertive. For example, it may be telling your spouse or boss what you really think about some issue or perhaps being able to return merchandise at a store. It may be one of the issues in the Assertiveness Self-Rating scale on page 99.

2. What would you usually do or expect from yourself in the situation? Has it worked?

3. What else could you do? Make a list of at least three alternatives.

4. If you did any of these alternatives, what are three Possible Positive Outcomes of each alternative?

5. Which Possible Positive Outcomes would probably have the most favorable long-range consequences?

Maximize your energy! Assertiveness is a freeing-up of your energy toward power. It is positive energy-charging rather than negative energy-draining. People admire assertive women. You can be one of them.

5

MOTHERS, FATHERS
AND YOUR SELF-ESTEEM

We get our first boosters—and squashers—from our parents. Most mothers and fathers have encouraged happy, constructive behaviors in their daughters as they grow up. However, sometimes we get split messages: boosters from one parent and squashers from the other. One parent may help our self-esteem rise and the other parent may push it down. We have all experienced a variety of parenting styles and so each of our experiences in growing up is unique and so are the dimensions of our self-esteem.

As you read this chapter, try to recall the boosters and squashers you received from your parents and how they affected your feelings about your "self." If you see yourself—or your parents—in some of the stories in this chapter, don't blame your parents. They did the best they could. We point out some common themes and patterns to help you understand why your self-esteem level is what it is and where you may have acquired some of your behaviors.

As you grow up, relationships with your parents change. Now that you are older, if you are fortunate, you love your parents as parents *and* friends. Unfortunately, others become alienated from their parents and have very little contact with them as adults.

You may think about your parents in different ways now than you did when you were younger. Once you may have idolized them and wanted to be like them, or the opposite may be true. As you grow older, you have opportunities to see how other people interact with their parents and other styles of parenting. You may have read self-help books, taken relationship courses, and possibly undergone therapy. In this process, attitudes about yourself and your relationship with your parents may have changed, and for good reason: You have had more life experiences, have achieved some insights into your own behaviors, or you or your parents have changed.

If you are a mother, or if you hope to be one someday, there are many insights you can give your children (boys as well as girls) about power and self-esteem. How you express your own attitudes about yourself will influence them. As you develop a better understanding of where some of your own boosters or squashers came from, you become better equipped to empower yourself.

Where Womanpower Starts: Daughterpower

Daughterpower means that you grew up with an empowering level of self-esteem as a result of boosters from your parents. Most women form their basic sense of self before the age of ten. Messages they heard as little girls may have stuck with them as boosters, if they were lucky, or squashers, if they weren't so lucky.

Daughterpower means that you and your parents had mutual respect for each other and that you listened to each other. You were able to accept each others likes and dislikes, even when there was a difference of opinion. You were able to share joys and sorrows and trust each other with secrets. You were proud of each other and pleased to introduce the other to friends. You were given encouragement to make choices, take risks, and move forward with your life. You were praised for the good things you did, and when criticism was necessary, it was given and received in a good-humored spirit of love and constructiveness. If you have Daughterpower, you and your parents communicated openly and effectively with each other most of the time.

WHERE DO YOU STAND ON THE DAUGHTERPOWER SCALE?

You may be a teenager, or you may be a woman in her midlife. Chances are you will answer the following questions in a different way than you might have when you were younger. Answer them as you feel *now,* but think about changes you have made in your attitudes since you were younger.

If your mother and/or father are alive, you are fortunate. We hope that you will make the most of your relationship. If your mother and/or father are deceased, how would you have answered the questions during their lifetime? There are two separate questionnaires: one regarding your mother and one regarding your father. Choose one or both to answer. You may find it interesting to compare your answers from the two questionnaires. You may learn that like many other women, you received boosts from one parent but were "depowered" by the other.

Please check YES or NO to the questions. More YES answers mean that you grew up with Daughterpower. More NO answers mean that your power as a daughter needs a boost. You can use the four "A" steps of the Womanpower Boosting Cycle (page 68) to get going.

YOU AND YOUR MOTHER

	YES	NO
Does your mother say things you want to listen to?		
Do you feel your mother listens to you?		
Do you respect her opinions and attitudes?		
Do you accept her likes and dislikes if they differ from your own?		
Does your mother let you make your own choices and decisions?		
Does your mother support you in your decisions when they do not agree with her preferences?		
Do you ask for her opinion on your own issues?		
Can you discuss "emotionally charged" issues with your mother?		
Do you trust your mother with your secrets?		
Do you share your joys with her?		
Does she do the same with you?		
Is your mother the first person you go to if you have any trouble?		

	YES	NO
Are you the first person your mother goes to if she has good news?		
Do you value your mother's opinion about clothes you choose for yourself?		
Do you feel valued and important by your mother?		
Do you feel loved by your mother?		
Are you proud of your mother and the way she looks?		
Are you usually pleased to introduce your friends to your mother?		
Do you think your mother generally likes your friends?		
Does your mother encourage you to make new friends?		
Does your mother encourage you to move forward in your life?		
Does your mother share recipes with you?		
Does your mother let you do things your way in the kitchen?		
Did your mother praise your accomplishments at school or work?		
Do you enjoy your mother's company?		

	YES	NO
Do you consider yourselves good friends?		

YOU AND YOUR FATHER

	YES	NO
Does your father say things you want to listen to?		
Do you feel your father listens to you?		
Do you respect his opinions and attitudes?		
Do you accept his likes and dislikes if they differ from your own?		
Does your father let you make your own choices and decisions?		
Does your father support you in your decisions when they are not in concurrence with his preferences?		
Do you ask for his opinion on your own issues?		
Can you discuss "emotionally charged" issues with your father?		
Do you trust your father with your secrets?		
Do you share your joys with him?		
Does he do the same with you?		

	YES	NO
Is your father the first person you go to if you have any trouble?		
Are you the first person your father goes to if he has good news?		
Do you value your father's opinion about clothes you choose for yourself?		
Do you feel valued and important by your father?		
Do you feel loved by your father?		
Are you proud of your father and the way he looks?		
Are you usually pleased to introduce your friends to your father?		
Do you think your father generally likes your friends?		
Does your father encourage you to make new friends?		
Does your father encourage you to move forward in your life?		
Does your father share sports/hobbies/interests with you?		
Does your father let you do things your way?		
Did your father praise your schoolwork? Grades?		

	YES	NO

Do you enjoy your
father's company?

Do you consider
yourselves good friends?

Scoring Yourself

If you answered YES to most of the above questions, you received lots of booster messages. Because we are most impressionable in our early years, when we get our first boosters and squashers, those often stick with us the longest. Your mother and father were loving and nurturing and encouraged your self-esteem, and you are moving ahead effectively with what you want out of life.

If you answered NO to more than six questions, chances are you may have been short-changed in the self-esteem department and need more boosters now. If you were one of the lucky girls, you received many boosters. If you didn't, you may have been hurting or feeling gypped for a long time.

Reviewing your answers to the above quizzes will help you understand why you have some of your attitudes and behaviors regarding self-esteem.

Parents Influence Self-Esteem in Many Ways

Women's relationships with their fathers can take many forms. Some girls idolize their fathers and believe that they do everything right. However, many such girls grow up with unrealistic expectations of men. They may feel frustrated when their husbands don't meet their idealized version of Dad. Still other women prefer men very unlike their fathers, because their fathers weren't present or emotionally available to them. Some women don't trust men because their fathers cheated on or abused their mothers.

Some girls grew up with aggressive, domineering and tyrannical fathers, while other girls grow up with absent fathers who abandoned the family or divorced their mothers. Some girls grew up with abusive fathers; the girls may have been sexually, physically, or emotionally abused and were forced to keep secrets from their mothers. Some fathers created jealousy between the daughter and the mother. We know of one father who takes his daughter out socially, leaving the mother at home. He delights in "dating" his daughter and being seen with an attractive "younger woman."

All these types of behaviors by fathers influence young women, their views of men, reactions to men, and their adult relationships with men. For example, a girl with the tyrannical father may grow up to fear authority and become very passive, even in the workplace. A woman who was abused by her father may grow up to fear intimacy. She may equate love with pain and hurt. A girl who was abandoned by her father may fear intimacy because she equates love with being abandoned. Her self-esteem needs boosting.

Relationships between women and their mothers also take on many forms. Some women who admire their mothers want to emulate them, while others, who do not agree with their mothers' habits or outlooks, want to be as different as possible.

We know many mothers who strive for perfection in housekeeping. Some daughters who grew up in such a household realize that other activities, such as jogging, or taking music lessons, are more valuable than constant and excessive housework. Other daughters, however, constantly berate themselves for not having a house as clean/tidy/attractive as their mothers'.

Some young women who have super-achiever mothers feel frustrated because they can't seem to do as many things as their mothers. An example is our friend Vera, whose midlife mother is president of her church women's group, heads up a local fund-raising drive for retarded children, and still works full-time in a real estate office. Vera finds taking care of her young child and working part-time all she can do and wonders why she just isn't as productive as her busy mom.

Young women observe marital behaviors between their mothers and fathers. If the mother puts herself in a subservient role to the father, the girl may grow up thinking that's how marriage should be. On the other hand, with empowerment, she would say to herself, "that's not how I want my marriage to be."

Some of the stories in this chapter demonstrate how, in some cases, parents sap the girl's energy and power, and the girl feels powerless, unloved, unprotected, and that she has no ally. On the other hand, some girls grow up in families with emotionally healthy parents and still have low self-esteem. For example, girls may get unintentional squashers from comparisons with siblings or others. The self-defeating messages that linger on are, "You just don't measure up" or "They are better than you are." For many reasons, some girls just feel different than their peers. This may happen to some whose parents were poor, lived "on the wrong side of the tracks," or speak with heavy foreign accents. This may happen to some who were brought up by one parent, relatives, or by foster parents. It can happen because of your place in the family (birth order) or any one of many other circumstances.

Some girls are aware that their parents wanted a boy first. Historically, in agrarian cultures, boys were considered necessary to do the heavy work on the farm. Somehow this notion has lingered in many parental heads. What happens in many families is that they may give their first-born a boy's name, treat her as a boy, and tell her she was a "mistake" and not what they wanted. This makes a girl feel very unimportant and reduces her self-esteem.

In some families, boys are sent to college, but the

girls are not. This differentiation reduces a girl's self-esteem. It says to her, "I'm not important. I'm not as good as my brother."

Here are some stories many of you may relate to.

How Some Women Boosted Their Self-Esteem

Comparisons, real or perceived, can squash a girl's self-esteem. For example, a girl who grows up in a family with one or more sisters and is constantly compared in an unfavorable way to a sister can be quashed. Here's what happened to Rena:

> As I was growing up, my parents always raved about how pretty my sister was. She was four years older and very popular in school. My parents spent a lot of money on having her photograph taken in glamorous poses. They always pointed out how beautiful she looked in pictures. They didn't have my picture taken as often, and when they did, they never put it out in a frame. What message do you think I got from all this?

Rena married, raised two daughters, and at 40 was divorced. She didn't wear makeup and went to her secretarial job at a car dealership in sweat clothes. "Why bother?" she said. "I'm not pretty and no one will notice how I look anyway." That was before she decided to change her ways. She followed the four "A" steps toward self-esteem in this way:

Awareness: Rena realized when her parents praised her sister's looks, she interpreted their praise to mean "I'm not pretty." Rena took a close look in the mirror. She thought her skin looked quite nice and that her features were good. She *could* be attractive with a little more effort.

Acceptance: She accepted the fact that her appearance and choice of clothing for work had been *her own* decision.

Alternatives: Rena realized that her choices included to continue not wearing makeup and wearing sweat clothes or to dress more like the other women, in tailored pants suits and nice dresses. She began watching department-store ads for free makeup demonstrations. She asked other women at work where they shopped for attractive, affordable clothes.

Action: The real turning point came when Rena spent a Saturday trying out makeup, buying several products, and shopping. She bought several outfits for work that she felt good in.

Rena started wearing her new clothes to work and got many compliments from her co-workers. She began to feel good about herself. Now she thinks about how her own attitudes and habits may have affected *her* daughters' self-esteem and appearance, and she encourages them to take a better look at themselves and make some changes, too.

Many girls develop personality traits because of what goes on in their families. For example, they may become placating "good girls," looking for positive strokes, or rebellious just to get noticed, even if being noticed results in negative strokes. Some learn to trust one or the other parent or to fear one or the other parent.

While many women want to be like their mothers when they grow up, others want to be the total opposite, like Claudia, who is 29 and married.

When I was a little girl, the most important thing to my mother was what other people thought. She emphasized being and looking perfect at all times. She vacuumed her white carpet every day, just in case anyone dropped in. She put me in dresses when other kids were wearing play clothes, and even then criticized my appearance. She looked upon the house and my appearance as a reflection on her. She considered my grades in school a reflection on her, too. I got really good grades, but no matter what I did, I just didn't measure up. "Not good enough," she often said. So I stopped trying. Then she called me "the rebel." Once I had a fantasy of rolling in the mud, and then rolling on her white carpet just to get back at her.

I listened to the squashers she gave me. When you're little and vulnerable and parents are your caretakers, you don't see their problems. You don't know then that they are vulnerable, too.

My father, on the other hand, praised my good looks, good grades, and successes in school and encouraged me to go after what I wanted out of life. I've learned that I can be strong and still be feminine like a woman without accepting my mother's values. I've chosen which qualities I want from both of my parents. Sad to say, I never considered my mother as a friend. I felt badly about that.

Here's how Claudia used the four "A" steps and became empowered:

Awareness: First she achieved insight into understanding her mother's sense of values. Claudia's mother liked everything "perfect," probably because of the way she had been raised. The mother regarded Claudia's appearance in play clothes as a blemish on *her own* perfection. She couldn't stand Claudia going to the store with her in blue jeans because it drew attention to *her* as possibly defective in some way.

Acceptance: Claudia accepted the fact that she and her mother were two different individuals and that each was entitled to her own beliefs and habits.

Alternatives: She realized that she and her mother, now about 65, could communicate if they just stayed away from certain subjects, like housekeeping and clothing. And she now can say to her mother, "That's how you do things. I do them my way."

Claudia says: "I was lucky. I realized, after following the four "A" steps, that most of my mother's criticisms made no sense and were gross exaggerations. Also I remember that my dad would tell me to ignore a lot of what my mother said. This saved me."

Action: As a parent, I decided to be much more relaxed about housekeeping. My four-year-old daughter has toys all over the house. I don't mind. The important aspects of our lives are in order: We communicate well. Even though she's still little, I praise her a lot and encourage her to develop her personal strengths. She's very outgoing and kids like her.

Pleasing Parents: Gloria the Good

Gloria is 25 years old. She was born eighteen months after her brother, who had minimal brain damage and later became hyperactive and required special education and constant attention from her parents. Early on, she made a decision to please her parents to make up for the trouble they had with her brother. She did not want to burden her parents with any of her concerns. So she became a "good" girl, perfect in every way, a high-achiever in school and socially popular. Throughout college, she and her parents planned for her to go to law school. Along the way, she changed her mind but was afraid to tell her parents, especially her father. She found her mother easier to approach and asked her, "Will Dad be devastated if I don't apply to a law school? Will you tell him?" Because of years of always doing what she thought her parents wanted her to, Gloria was nervous about telling her parents about her own life choices. But Gloria decided to change her life. By using the four "A" steps, here's how she did it:

Awareness: She realized that though it was okay to want to please her parents, she shouldn't think that she could buy their love by being what they wanted.

Acceptance: She learned to accept the fact that her parents love her anyway, even if she doesn't choose a law career.

Alternatives: She considered what other career choices she was prepared for and what interested her.

Action: After working through these steps, Gloria was able to discuss her career choices with her dad. She was honest and open about her feelings regarding law school. He listened to her concerns and her other interests. He agreed that she has a good head for business and that going for an MBA degree and looking toward an executive position, possibly in marketing, would be a good choice.

If you are a parent, the lesson from Gloria is: Let your daughter be who she wants to be.

Hand-Me-Down Hannah

Some women acquire their sense of self-esteem from unintentional messages from their parents. Consider Hannah, a young woman who only got hand-me-down clothes:

My parents were married early in the depression. They bought nice clothes for my sister. I was three years younger, so I got them after she outgrew them. "We're so glad you are a girl so we don't have to buy you new clothes," they told me. I never felt important enough to make my own choices about my clothes. I always felt self-conscious in my sister's old clothes, although they were usually nice things and fit okay. Now I feel a compulsion to shop in resale or discount shops and not spend much money on my own clothes or other things for myself. I grew up thinking I didn't deserve things. This has been a hard squasher to overcome, and money now isn't the problem.

Here's how Hannah boosted her feelings about her self-worth with the four "A"s:

Awareness: Hannah is aware that her compulsion to shop only in resale shops comes from her past. She knows she can afford items from other places. She also is aware that she deserves to make her own choices about where she shops.

Acceptance: Hannah says that her habit now is of her own doing. She has chosen this method of purchasing, even though she doesn't feel good about it.

Alternatives: Hannah's choices are fairly clear. She can choose to change her methods of shopping, or use a combination of sources, including some resale shops.

Action: Hannah began her new shopping plan by reviewing some upscale women's clothing catalogues to see what they were showing. Then she visited several department stores and women's specialty stores. She realized that her habit of scouting resale shops isn't all bad and that she may continue to do so for some items. However, for her regular wardrobe, she will shop department stores, and particularly watch for sales.

Hannah feels good about herself for making these new decisions. She doesn't feel guilty spending money for clothes for herself. She can afford it, and, she tells herself, "I deserve it."

Irene: Don't Leave Me, Too!

Irene, now 37, grew up as the only child in a single-parent household with her divorced mother. She feels very close to her mother, but not to her father. Her mother had always encouraged her to go after what she wants and to set her sights high. Her father, on the other hand, had always browbeaten her with, "You can't do anything right. You don't make the right choices unless I make them for you." Here's what Irene says:

I was young when my parents divorced. I remember thinking I better be nice to Daddy or he will leave me, just like he left Mommy. Throughout my school years, I regularly spent time with Dad on weekends and during vacations. After college I announced my independence, took a job and moved south. I'm very close to my mother, talk to her, see her often, and share secrets with her. Sometimes I'd tell her, "Don't tell Dad . . . I couldn't tell Dad this . . ." I realized that I still wanted to be the "perfect daughter" to assure that Dad will continue to love me.

Through the years, Irene's mother has encouraged her to keep up the contact with her father, although there are many times Irene doesn't want to see him because of the criticism she endures from him. He continues to be domineering even though Irene is now grown up. When he sees her several times a year, which involves a lengthy plane trip for either of them, he criticizes her appearance, her clothes, or the man she is seeing, and rarely gives an honest compliment or word of praise. He expects her to be with him on his birthday, no matter what her work schedule is at that time. If she doesn't do as he asks, he makes her feel guilty. His constant badgering still bothers her so much that she often cries after a visit with him. Irene's steps toward self-esteem were:

Awareness: Irene now has a new awareness of the truth of her situation, which is that her Dad would still love her, even if he knew the secrets she sometimes shares with her mother. And she realizes that if she could speak honestly with her Dad about the way she feels about his constant barrage of squashers, she might feel freer, and perhaps he would lighten up on his constant verbal assault.

Acceptance: Irene realizes that she is stuck in her situation in large part because she has never stood up for her rights. Irene needs to stand up to her father and simply say, "I'm an adult now. When you talk to me like a child, I feel badly." She is aware of the effect he has on squashing her self-esteem. She has permitted him to continue his abuse because she retains those "rubber band" messages in her head that tell her, "If I'm not what he wants, he'll leave me, too." Irene now knows how to be assertive and take this position. In Chapter 4, she read about assertiveness and some suggestions for coping. For example, when her father is critical of the way she looks, she might say to him, "What is it about my appearance that you don't like?"

Alternatives: Irene's alternatives were fairly straightforward. Either stay stuck or become more assertive. She chose assertiveness.

Action: Now, when Irene is annoyed by her father's comments, she lets him know. Irene has worked through the four "A" steps of the Womanpower Boosting Cycle and continues to work on changing some of her long-held, self-defeating messages. Irene knows that she is lovable, capable, and attractive, despite what she hears from her father. She also knows that he will always be her father and love her, despite what choices in life she makes, and thus far in matters that count, she has made good choices.

Cynthia's Message: You Can't Count on Others

Cynthia is 42 years old. She is very independent, so independent that she has not been able to develop a close relationship with a man. Cynthia tells all:

My mother was ill a lot when I was a little girl. Since I was five years old, I remember her staying in her bedroom a lot of the time. My father put his energy into taking care of her. He encouraged me to be a good girl so that Momma would be okay. I did a lot of work around house that mothers usually do. I tried to be good, hoping she would get better, but my mother never got better and I never got any more strokes from her. I felt like a trapped slave with squashed self-esteem. I had no one to count on. As I grew up, I believed that you can only count on yourself. Other people always let you down.

Along with this emotional baggage, Cynthia got very fat at an early age and was teased at school, which made her feel terrible about herself. She was always the last one chosen for gym teams. Now Cynthia has trouble keeping an intimate relationship going because she doesn't trust that anyone really cares about her. The early stages of relationships are fine, but she fears that being loved won't last. She feels

unprotected, and that she has no ally. She has no
inner support system.

With the help of women friends, Cynthia worked
through the four "A" steps, realizing that she can
trust others. She took *action* with her life and now has
a happy relationship with a man.

Mona the Mouse

> *My mother has been an alcoholic for as long as I
> can remember. My father was absent from home
> a lot of the time. I got no love and attention from
> anyone. I was afraid to come home from school
> because when my mother had been drinking, she
> would rage at me and berate me. She was critical
> and verbally abusive and would even awaken me
> in the middle of the night to shout at me for no
> good reason. I became shy and quiet in school. I
> avoided getting into any kind of trouble. I be-
> lieved that if you upset people, they get crazy and
> hurt you.*
>
> *I became known as "Little Mouse." I felt that I
> had no friends. I was ashamed of my mother and
> embarrassed by her. I had no one to turn to. Even
> at home, I felt unsafe and unprotected.*

As an adult, Mona kept the same job for years, even
though she knew she was capable of doing better. She
couldn't trust anyone, either in business or personal
relationships. Mona is a very attractive woman. She is
an example of one who has good looks but because of
squashed self-esteem and lack of self-confidence sees
herself as someone who has to hide not only herself
but her feelings as well.

Mavis: Effects of Overprotective Parents

> *I'm Mavis and I'm 36. My hearing loss and
> learning disability was diagnosed during first
> grade. My mother was overprotective. As I grew*

*up, I interpreted her protectiveness as a lack of
trust. I thought that if she trusted me as she
trusted my sister, she'd let me be independent.
Until recently, I was furious with my mother.
Now I realize that her protectiveness was out of
love.*

Olivia: Engulfed by Mother

*I'm Olivia. I'm 35 and alone. I'll describe my
mother as an octopus. When I was little, my
father was warm, loving, and held me and kissed
me a lot. I really loved him. When I was eleven,
he had a business setback, lost his business, and
out of frustration became less affectionate to both
me and my mom. What a shock, from loving to
absolute coldness. Mom moved into another bedroom. She made me her surrogate husband. She
never let me go out with friends. She couldn't
stand my being a separate individual from her.
She didn't believe in divorce because of her
religious convictions. She wanted me to replace
my dad. As a teenager and young adult, she
objected to my dating. When I was old enough
and could get a job, I moved across the country to
get away from her tentacles.*

*Now I'm afraid of intimacy. I can't seem to
bond with men or women. I think, if men are nice
and loving, I can't trust them. I got that idea from
my father. And my roommate tells me I'm engulfing her. I seem to be driving her away, too.*

Olivia has been "engulfing" her roommate by being
demanding and giving her a hard time if she wants to
do anything on her own. What has happened is that
Olivia has ended up being very much like the parent
from whom she wanted to be different. Olivia has an
incomplete self. To fill the void, she fills up with part
of the other person. Now Olivia pushes men and

women away. She is afraid of and doesn't trust nice men and engulfs women.

Self-Esteem and Sexuality

Ideally, young women get their attitudes and information about sexuality from their parents or from education in school. Unfortunately, this doesn't always happen. Some learn about sexuality from older men who mistreat them or from other unhealthy sources. Because they have felt unloved at home, they seek what they perceive as a place in which they will be accepted. Some women rebel against their early loveless home life by adopting addictive behaviors, such as drugs, eating disorders, or sexual promiscuity.

"I've seen many teenage girls, who felt unloved at home "acting out" sexually to get attention. "They think the way to be admired is to be sexually active with a boyfriend, instead of doing well in school," says Pamela A. Mohr from the Center on Children and the Law at the American Bar Association, Washington, D.C. "Many of these girls have babies. Some go back to school and get their GED diploma. Some schools have programs for teenage mothers. That's a good thing, when the young Moms keep their babies and can have day care right at school for the infants. It helps both of them. There should be more places that make it available instead of socially and educationally 'punishing' the girls."

Susie's Story

My mother was very closemouthed about sex. I remember once she saw that I had my hand in my panties. She had a fit that I was "touching myself down there." As I got older she never answered any questions about sex and my body. Later I started exploring with girls and boys. I became a

*total rebel. I would show myself, looking for
attention sexually. You might say I became promiscuous.*

To help herself outgrow her early messages and
habits, Susie sought counseling. Still in psychotherapy, Susie is now trying to maintain a relationship
with a young man. She hopes that the relationship
will last.

Love Causes Pain: JoAnn's Story

*My father died before I was born. My mother was
depressed. As I was growing up, she told me that I
was unwanted. I don't remember ever being
hugged or held. I was often left in my crib, crying,
and no one came. Later, in an effort to find love, I
became sexually promiscuous and looked for
boys with whom to have sexual relationships,
mistaking this attention for love, but in the long
run, causing pain.*

A strong amount of willpower and determination,
as well as psychotherapy with a therapist JoAnn
trusts, is helping her.

Divorce in the Family and Self-Esteem

At the end of the twentieth century, with divorce
rates increasing, many young women find their self-
esteem squashed because they are "caught in the
middle" of divorcing parents. An increasing number
of children must adjust to being in "split" families.
Many grow up feeling doubts about themselves, including their own lovability, that they may be at fault
in causing the divorce, and that there is the possibility
of being left by a parent.

Sometimes daughters of divorced mothers "inher-
it" ideas from their mothers. Some have mothers who

hate men. Some mothers bad-mouth their ex-hus-bands, and the daughters grow up thinking that men are "no good."

Issues of trust are high on the list of concerns of children of divorce. Many grown-up children in di-vorced families ask themselves, "What can I count on?" and "Can I ever trust anyone?"

If children are young, they need reassurance and reinforcement from both parents that they are loved, that they had no part in causing the divorce, and that they will not be left. If the children are older, major issues dividing the parents may be discussed. Chil-dren are aware of personality characteristics; they may have grown up seeing the rift between their parents long before the parents announced their im-pending divorce.

Boost Your Daughters

If you received a lot of nurturing boosters, then you probably tend to be encouraging of your children. The supportive parent provides "the model" for her chil-dren, and influences them. Nurturing leads to the empowered, happier child.

If you are a mother working on your own Woman-power Boosting Cycle, your daughter will see and experience it, too. Share your thoughts with her. Let her know what you like and don't like about yourself. Let her know what scares you; let her in on your vulnerabilities. Be proud of yourself and your accomp-lishments. Let her know.

Ada's Influence on Her Daughter, Ruth

I gave boosters to Ruth, now 36, as she grew up. The result is good. She is a lawyer practicing in Los Angeles. She says that I have been an impor-tant influence in boosting her self-esteem and giving her the courage to do the things she wanted. After graduating from a midwestern law school, Ruth wanted to move to the West Coast. What better time is there to make a geographical change than when one is just starting a career? she asked. I agreed. But the California bar examination is so difficult, Ruth said. My reply: "You can do it." She passed the California bar examination on her first try. She made new friends, and developed new hobbies, including skiing, sailing and scuba diving, then met and married a wonderful man.

Now some of Ruth's friends tell her they would like to do new things—change jobs, enter a tennis tournament, learn another language, or sign up for a tour abroad. Some say they just can't make themselves do these things, but they admire how Ruth just goes after what she wants. She takes action because she has had enough boosters to feel good about herself.

Sheila's Influence on Her Daughter, Laurie

Laurie, now 30, says that my influence, as well as her father's, added to her personality and capabilities. Laurie believes that hearing about my struggle to overcome my physical handicap gave her a deep sense of determination. She says, "I learned to go after what I wanted in life. Raised in such an environment, I took for granted that women can achieve as much as men. This not only enhanced my determination, but also gave me an increased sense of independence and confidence."

Some mothers don't want to show their vulnerability. Children then think their mothers are "perfect," and try too hard to emulate them—or feel frustrated and rebel. Let your daughter know that you don't consider yourself perfect and that you don't expect her to be that way, either.

Encourage your daughter to talk freely with her father, if possible, as well as to you. Getting a male perspective can help a young woman develop a more realistic viewpoint of the real-world life.

Be aware that your own mother's problems don't have to become your problems. Accept responsibility for your own actions. Consider your alternatives and take action. Learn to separate rather than internalize your mother's problems. Separate from her lack of power, if powerlessness is her trait. It need not be yours.

If you have controversies with your own parents, share those thoughts with your daughter. If you and she have differences of opinions, acknowledge the validity of her feelings. Discuss your differences openly, without criticism or judgment. Become friends. Like each other. It will help build Woman-power.

6

GETTING CLOSE:
RELATIONSHIPS AND INTIMACY

Relationships come in all sizes and strengths. We all have many types of relationships throughout our lives. We have relationships with parents, siblings, and other relatives. Relationships occur with friends, and more complicated relationships occur with those with whom we are sexually intimate.

We have friendships in which we share common interests—we may have tennis friends, bridge partners, or fellow students in a class. We also have more personal and intimate relationships, such as with a parent or child, or dating or living together relationships.

What Is Intimacy?

Intimacy is when you allow yourself to be close, open, and honest, and to trust another. It is when you share yourself, let yourself be vulnerable, and take down your barriers. It is a feeling of bonding with another.

There are various degrees of intimacy. For example, the closeness you may feel with a good friend, parent, or child is very different from the closeness you feel toward a lover or spouse. With some relationships, intimacy seems a very natural step. The more you trust someone, the more willing you are to let your guard down.

Many feel very content and comfortable in intimate relationships. Those are women who most likely feel lovable and can trust being loved and close to another. Their positive self-talk sounds like this:

I am lovable

I deserve to be loved

I can trust closeness

Intimacy feels good

On the other hand, those women who don't feel lovable, who don't trust that anyone would stay with them, and fear that a man can hurt them, have much more difficulty staying in or even forming an intimate relationship. They tend to run or get scared off when the closeness begins. Some don't even bother because they figure "who will love me and want to be with me anyway."

The "fear of intimacy" messages are negative self-defeating messages, the opposite of positive self-talk messages described above. Some examples of "fear of intimacy" self-talk messages are:

- I don't deserve to be loved.
- I can't trust anyone.
- People are mean to me.
- I don't belong.
- Men can hurt me.
- Men will control me (I feel trapped).
- It won't last anyway.
- I am not good enough, no one will want me.

Many women and men who were victims of sexual molestation or severe psychological abuse at an early age may have these fears.

TEST YOURSELF ON INTIMACY

Are you happy with your intimate relationships? Or are you one of many women who want to begin recognizing your own lovability to improve your relationships and your self-esteem?

Which of the following statements sound like you? Those in the left column or those in the right column, or some of both? Respond to each statement with a Yes or No answer.

Intimacy feels good to me. ____	Being close to others scares me. ____
Closeness with another brings me a feeling of inner warmth and contentment. ____	Letting my guard down can set me up to be hurt. ____
I can be open and honest about my real self with those I trust. ____	You really can't trust others; they can inflict a lot of pain. ____
I like to surround myself with special friends with whom I can freely share my personal self. ____	Intimacy means always having to please someone else. ____
Connecting to others in an intimate relationship is a very important part of my life. ____	Intimacy means being responsible for someone else. ____
I feel safe sharing my real self with my intimate partner. ____	I can't trust my real feelings to others because they can use them against me. ____

> If I let my guard down
> in an intimate
> relationship, he/she can
> use it to control and
> manipulate me. I'll lose
> my freedom. _____

Do you find yourself answering YES to more of the questions in the column at the right? Are you afraid of intimacy? What aspect of intimacy frightens you? Many women long for intimacy. Yet for many, intimacy doesn't always happen easily. Many find it difficult to develop and keep close relationships. Are you one of them? What gets in your way?

Perhaps out of fear you are either stuck in an unhealthy relationship or not in one at all. It may help you to understand what types of relationships work best and what types do not work at all.

Healthy vs. Unhealthy Intimate Relationships

How can you tell if you have a healthy or unhealthy relationship? Following are four basic types of intimate relationships and how they are achieved. (These usually apply to couples but can also apply to roommates and friends.)

TYPES OF RELATIONSHIPS: A, B, C, D

$$A. \quad \frac{1}{2} + \frac{1}{2} \qquad\qquad = 1$$
$$B. \quad \frac{1}{2} + \frac{1}{2} \qquad\qquad = 2$$
$$C. \quad 1 + 1 \qquad\qquad = 2$$
$$D. \quad 1 + 1 + 1 = 3$$

Situation A

In Situation A, the individuals are symbiotic, which means that they are so connected to each other that each gives up something of himself or herself and the two become the whole ($\frac{1}{2} + \frac{1}{2} = 1$). This was more common among older generations because people depended on each other for survival. To many of these loving folks, marriage meant giving up part of the self. However, this may be not be the best for both partners; we need to maintain wholeness and be a whole self to survive on our own.

For years, many women sacrificed themselves to keep their men happy. They didn't even think about getting an education or having a career and did not develop a sense of self. Their career was housewife and mother. The man, on the other hand, depended on her to do all the household duties—cook, clean, and take care of children, If Mom wanted to go out, she had to clear it with Dad. He depended on her and she depended on him.

In this type of extremely interconnected relationship, it has not been unusual that when one of the partners dies, the other often dies shortly after. Or if one decides to leave the interdependent relationship because he/she feels too stifled, the other may panic because he/she has relied on the other for completeness. The last point has often been more true for older generation women whose role was wife and mother. If the husband died or left, the woman felt totally powerless to go on with her life. In fact, she would even continue to sign her name, Mrs. John Doe rather than Mary Doe. In the current generation, many married women do not give up their own last names. They keep their own identity, totally the opposite of their mothers. Some older widows keep their phones listed under their husband's name for years.

Some women who let their identity be swallowed up by their husbands are left powerless if their middle-aged husbands leave them for younger women. Many are left devastated; sometimes without income, often without self.

Here's what Sheila says about overly dependent relationships:

If during counseling I recognize a relationship based on overly mutual dependency, I work

> *with each of the partners to try to complete their own wholeness, to help them feel their own individual power and then bring that individual power to strengthen the relationship. That way, if either partner leaves because of death or other reasons, the person being left will feel whole and powerful and know he/she can handle life on his/her own."*

Situation B

In Situation B, the 1½ is dominant, and the ½ is submissive (1½ + ½ = 2). Co-dependent, non-assertive or abusive relationships fall into this category. The one who is in the passive, submissive role has often been the woman. However, with women becoming stronger and feeling their power, many no longer want to be in this kind of unequal partnership. This then threatens the man, who gets his power by keeping his partner submissive.

"Women are the weaker sex" used to be a common myth. Now we know this is far from the truth and never was really the case. While many men may be physically larger and stronger, they are not necessarily emotionally stronger than women. However, the woman who allowed herself to be dominated, controlled, and easily intimidated, was the "good girl" all along. She has to please at all costs. Chances are, this woman, as a little girl, may have felt unloved, unimportant, unwanted, dumb, stupid, or not worth much. Her opinions may not have been acknowledged or heard. She may have lived with alcoholic or divorced parents, or in a home in which she felt and took the brunt of the pain.

Sadly, many of us tend to repeat previous patterns of relationships even if they felt terrible, because that is what we know. That's our comfort zone—until we see the situation as it really is.

Awareness can change your outlook. You can reduce your submissiveness and replace it with Woman-power once you realize that you do not have to sacrifice your soul to be loved. You deserve to be a whole self, with feelings and opinions. You deserve to be heard and acknowledged. You do not have to allow yourself to be controlled or dominated. You should have an equal share in the relationship. Use the first of the 4 "A" steps—Awareness. Become aware of what is going on in your life.

You can be assertive. This change is already going on everywhere—at home and at work. Secure men appreciate the shift in women's sense of themselves, while insecure men are threatened and seem to have trouble with assertive, "whole" women.

Situation C

In situation C, the 1 + 1 live as "married singles," with very little interaction. Each go their separate ways. Neither is willing to give up anything or share with the other. This is really a very lonely kind of relationship. Many stay in this married-single relationship out of fear of leaving and being on their own, while others do it out of convenience. They may not be able to afford two households. They may want to stay together until the children are old enough to be on their own. On the one hand, this can be good, but on the other, very damaging, particularly if there is a lot of tension, conflict, and fighting, which can lead to pain for all in the household. These couples really should look at the consequences of staying together.

The Ideal: Situation D

The healthiest relationship which can lead to real intimacy and closeness for both parties is situation D, in which 1 + 1 + 1 = 3. There is Me, You, and Us. No one gives up any of himself or herself. There is equal sharing. "I'm all of Me and You are all of You.

Together, we are Us. We bond and connect. There is Me, You, and Our Relationship." This is something to strive for. These relationships are possible if we both bring a healthy, empowered sense of ourselves to the relationship. We respect ourselves and our partners. We accept the partnership as an equal sharing—with trust and mutual respect and love.

The happiest relationships, whether marriages, parent–child relationships, or friendships that work this way are the most satisfying and empowering for all concerned. These relationships boost self-esteem.

Why Do Women Stay in Unhealthy Relationships?

Women share some common reasons for getting into and staying in unhealthy relationships. Many have a fear of closeness, a poor perception of their own body image, or attribute their intimacy problems to parental warnings or religious upbringing.

There are common qualities in unhealthy relationships: fear of being alone, codependency, abuse, feelings of being trapped, overexpectations of marriage or divorce, involvement with a narcissistic partner, playing the "rescuer" role, feeling society's pressure toward marriage, or the long-lasting effects of early childhood abuse.

Some women are anxious or panic-stricken if they let others get too close. There are many reasons why women fear and therefore prevent intimacy. They may be afraid of being hurt, abused, engulfed, controlled or manipulated. Many are afraid of excessive fighting, pain, or being a victim. Many fear giving up freedom and decision-making power. They fear giving up theirselves (which is not exclusive to women). Sadly, many women do not feel lovable. They are not sure they deserve to be loved.

Girls who know what it's like to be loved and have seen their parents sharing a loving relationship with each other, generally find it easier and more natural to be in and maintain loving, close relationships as adult women. On the other hand, if as a child in your household, you experienced tension, abuse, excessive criticism, yelling, hurt, pain, battering, neglect, shame, or early abandonment, chances are it will be very scary and difficult for you to trust, bond, and open up to others.

Childhood Influences Stick with Us

Many women who have had an abusive, abandoning, overly fearful alcoholic or depressed parent become aware later in their life that their ability for intimacy was squashed when they were young. Some children who were abandoned equate love with "being left" and tend to avoid intimacy to avoid abandonment again. Children of alcoholics can't count on love and intimacy because of their parents' intermittent binges and consequent emotional or physical unavailability.

Children who grow up with an overly fearful parent who says things like, "Don't play near the street. I'm too scared," grow up with fears of negative outcomes, worrying all the time. This can stifle closeness.

Sharon

When I was very young, it was much easier for me to be close and trusting of men than women, especially attractive women, because my Dad was so loving and supportive, while Mom was always critical, judgmental, and never pleased. Now, my present-day expectation and perceptions of others, especially men, is a bounce back (rubber band) to how things were when I was a child.

Many young people grow up with overly critical parents. In some cases, regarding their mates, they become overcritical themselves. Unfortunately, mates frequently hear:

"Can't you do anything right?"

"He should do it my way. He should think of me first."

Growing up with either a very critical or self-involved parent can hurt a young girl's personal development of self-worth and self-value. While constantly being put down or constantly needing to "feed" the insecure parent, there is no positive reinforcer for her to build her own self-confidence. As an adult, she may feel self-doubt and insecurity, constantly seeing others as better than herself.

Molly's Memory

I don't want to be in a relationship. What can anyone ever give me? My mother talked about how sex was something men enjoyed and women endured. She never had nice things to say about my father. I never saw them being affectionate. She always criticized young men I dated and questioned me about how far we went.

Some women grow up believing the myth that nice women don't enjoy sexual activity, have sexual feelings, nor have wishes to express their sexual desires. Some women don't see themselves as sexual beings and therefore feel unattractive in a sexual way or are afraid of their own sexual desires. They think of themselves as cheap and sleazy. Some women were brought up to think of sexual activity as sinful, or at least something one engaged in only within marriage. When they discover enjoyment in sexual activity, they may feel guilty and that they are not "nice women." These feelings can really damage an intimate relationship.

Types of Unhealthy Relationships

Codependent Relationships

"I'm afraid to be alone. I live my life through him."

"I can't do it on my own."

"If I please him he'll change."

Codependency describes behaviors that get in the way of a healthy, equal relationship and squashes empowerment and self-esteem. For many women, their fear of being alone and not empowered keeps them in the unhealthy relationship. Staying in the relationship in many cases leads to self-destructive behaviors such as overeating, alcoholism, and emotional disorders such as anxiety and depression.

Codependency with another person is somewhat like an addiction to a drug; and the codependent's addiction is harmful to the relationship. Like food, drugs, or alcohol addiction, we stay in the relationship to avoid facing the anxiety or pain of separation and being alone.

The codependent often serves as an "enabler" to the alcoholic or drug addict because she hopes to help her partner. She operates under the myth, "If I am nice, good, and cater to him, he will change." She puts up with abuse in the relationship because she is afraid to leave and be on her own. This feeling of "I can't do it alone" is a feeling of powerless and hopelessness. With this kind of individual, it is important for her to realize that she cannot change her partner and that she does not have to put up with abuse. She needs to learn to feel her own power and realize that she CAN do it alone and that the alcoholic spouse is not adding anything but pain to her life.

A woman who has an alcoholic husband makes excuses for his behavior and frequent non-participation in family or social situations. She avoids confrontation with him. She may say to the children, "Let's not upset Dad. Be good at dinnertime so that he doesn't get angry and drink a lot tonight." The woman sacrifices some of herself so as not to upset her husband. She is reactive not proactive.

Codependents hide their feelings and feel guilty when they do express themselves. They find that their moods depend on the moods of the other. They care about the other, but ignore their own needs, or lie to others to cover up for what is not right in the family. The result is squashed self-esteem.

A codependent relationship is a ½ + 1½. Being the small half docsn't fccl good. Codependency encourages the feeling of **entrapment.** For example, a woman in a codependent relationship sometimes asks herself, "If I left him, where would I go? Who else would have me?" She feels guilty for even thinking of leaving him. She may think he will start behaving in a better way toward her. While she may think about leaving him, she feels that if she leaves him, he may not support her financially, he may go further with his addiction and become seriously ill, or he may threaten suicide. Such codependent women have low self-esteem because they sacrificed their lives for their mates. They never developed a life of their own. An "entrapped" woman is in a ½ + 1 ½ relationship. This woman feels powerless and stuck. She is a "victim," living inside of her own self-constructed cocoon.

Women in codependent situations can work through the four "A" steps toward Womanpower. Consideration of alternatives and actions is a "must" for them.

Here's what Connie the Codependent Says:

We grew up together and got married when we were very young. He became a successful stockbroker. I taught junior college. We were emotion-

ally interdependent until he started having affairs. I shrugged them off, afraid of what I thought was my only alternative: being alone. I was angry and resentful. I denied what was going on and felt miserable. I became physically sick due to my angry feelings. I became bulimic. I was afraid he would leave me. Part of me wants him to go. He threatens to leave but never left. He's still here.

Maria and Jim: The Married Singles (Codependency)

Some couples stay together in a 1 + 1 relationship that never equals 2. Maria and Jim are in their late 50s. He runs a successful business and is active in the community. She is a volunteer at a local school. He is psychologically abusive to Maria when they are alone. He berates her, belittles her, and makes her feel unwanted and unloved. They have not shared any physical affection in years. When their son went off to college a few years ago, Jim moved into the son's room. Maria says:

He is often away from home in the evenings and on weekends. He tells me he is working or attending meetings. I really don't care where he is because I welcome the peace and solitude at home when he isn't there. I stay busy with my work and my friends. The only time we go out together socially is for "command performances" when he has to make an appearance with a wife for the community. For years, I thought about getting a divorce. First I told myself to wait until our son was grown up. Now I feel financially dependent on Jim. He owns the house, which is in his name alone. I don't have any money in my name. What can I do?

Engulfment

> *Anna: "If I get too close he will try to control me,
> have a hold on me, and I'll lose myself."*

Like Anna, many may fear being consumed, engulfed, or trapped in a relationship, losing freedom to
be oneself, and thus they avoid attachments. They
will allow just so much closeness, and then, if a
relationship turns into a commitment, they run.

Helene, 34, fears engulfment by love because she
grew up with an overly protective mother. She fears
that any intimate relationship will consume her, just
as her mother did. She can't be free because she fears
being trapped.

Early Abandonment

Jill's Story

Abandonment may be physical or psychological. It
may mean feeling rejected by one or more parents and
may lead to a lack of trust at an early age.

> *You can't trust men to stay with you. One way or
> another they go away and you are left on your
> own. Men come and go. My father and two
> brothers were killed in a car accident. My mother
> remarried; her second husband committed sui-
> cide. Mom married again, and then that man left
> her for a younger women. That's how I learned
> about the instability of relationships.*

After working through the four "A" steps and
seeing a therapist, Jill developed more self-confidence
and learned to be more trusting. The truth is that she
is a lovable person and chances are she will not repeat
her mother's pattern. She realizes that her mother's
situation was different from hers, and there is no

reason for her to adopt her mother's feelings as her own.

Diane and Her Alcoholic Dad

I'm 39 and not married. My mother was alcoholic and often drunk. My father was usually not at home. I don't trust that I'm lovable. When I meet men, I have a "DO" loop, to make them prove they love me. It's hard for them; I know I'm pushing them away. Many men give up. Then I say, "I knew I wasn't lovable. Why get close. It won't last anyway!

With sincere attention to the Awareness step in the four "A"s, Diane now realizes that her father's early abandonment of her was due to his alcoholism, not because he didn't love her. With development of more self-esteem, Diane now understands that she has much to offer and is indeed lovable. She will not make life so difficult for men who become attracted to her. She is ready for a healthy relationship.

Growing Up in an Abusive Household

Some girls grow up living with sexual abuse. Some develop the attitude that love equals pain and degradation, and thus stay away from love. It is fairly common for women who were abused as children to have a low sense of self-worth and not trust in intimate relationships.

Some girls grow up watching others being abused, particularly their mothers. They fear men hurting them or others. Here's Sue's story:

Men can be abusive tyrants. My dad was an army major and ran our household the same way. Mom was submissive, passive, and non-assertive. I saw Mom taking Dad's abuse, feeling powerless, as a victim, not doing anything to change things. As soon as you marry them, they think they can control you. I deliberately look for weak men I can control and push around, but then I leave them because I don't respect them.

Sue learned that all men do not have the characteristics of her father. She now knows that some men can be understanding, caring, and communicative. She now knows that her mother lacked the power to make any changes in her marriage. "What went on between the two of them shouldn't affect my choice of a mate," she now says.

The Caretaker

Frieda: The Family Fixer

Intimacy means I have to be responsible and take care of someone else. I don't want to do that. It's hard enough to take care of myself. When I was a little girl, both parents were out working a lot, and I felt like I had to hold down the fort and take care of my younger brothers. I had no childhood, no time for fun or to just be a kid. I don't want to get saddled with taking care of any man.

Frieda learned that intimacy can mean sharing as well as caring. She understands that in her relationships she need not be a caretaker.

Laura: The Parent to Everyone

I was the first of seven children. I, too, was the caretaker for my younger siblings, because my mother was often on alcoholic binges. I never really had a childhood. Life wasn't fair to me. I have a relationship with a man and I see myself "parenting" him; we both resent it. I hooked up with a man who needed parenting, because I was

*used to playing this role. Now I'm unhappy and
unfulfilled in this relationship.*

Like Frieda the Fixer, Laura the Parent has learned
through her Awareness step that she followed her old
pattern in choosing a lover, and the pattern didn't
produce a good result. Laura is becoming more open
in communicating with her man. They may work
things out or she may choose to be on her own. Laura
is thinking about alternatives without him and without the relationship.

Does any of this sound familiar? Could any of these
scenarios describe you or someone you know?

Women as "Settlers"

Rona's Story

Some women "settle" for less than they really want.
In many cases, "settling" comes from a lack of self-
esteem and sometimes explains early depression for
young women. Look at Rona the Settler:

*I was a "settler." I was a fat college freshman,
excited and thankful that Jack, attractive and
several years older, wanted to go out with me. At
age 19, I married Jack; I was afraid no other man
would want me. I wanted to finish college, but
Jack also wanted to go to graduate school. We
couldn't manage both educations financially. So
I worked and put off my own plans. His degree
took nine years. He got his degree and moved out
and across the country. We got divorced. I felt
used, abused, and manipulated. I had settled for
less and wound up with nothing—no husband, no
degree, and no money for my own education.*

Rona became an angry person. She acts out her
anger through substance addictions, which include

wine, food, and cigarettes. She had a very low estimation of herself and a feeling of powerlessness. Also, she realized that she had been a contributor to being used and manipulated.

With the four "A" steps, she dropped her addictive, destructive behaviors. She accepted some truths about herself: that she was a lovable, whole person, and that she could make it on her own. Eventually she completed her college degree and got a good job.

Women Who Marry Narcissistic Men (Gluttons for Punishment)

If I please him, then he will be good to me.

A woman married to a narcissistic man is in a ½ + 1½ situation.

The woman who chooses to marry the narcissist has to be passive and submissive and constantly feed her partner's bruised ego. The narcissist has to be stroked and pleased constantly.

To the outsider, the narcissist is often charming. It appears that the narcissist has an abundance of self-love. However, this usually is not the case. The truth is that this person needs to be constantly reassured, stroked, and pampered. He feeds on others, is self-absorbed, and interprets others' behaviors as either for or against him. So, if his wife has different opinions, he feels threatened, gets insecure, turns to anger, and tries to get his way by using aggressive behavior, making his wife feel wrong, stupid, and foolish.

The insecure woman, fearing his rage, feels guilty and tries to please him more, hoping he will be happy and love her. If she swallows herself and gives all to him, things may seem okay for a while until she just can't bear it anymore. Some get physically or emotionally ill in this situation. Many women in psychotherapy, while talking about their relationships with narcissistic men, say they get sick of feeding their men's egos without getting anything back.

If she becomes too strong, assertive, or powerful, the narcissist will feel scared, threatened, and intimidated. When the woman is assertive, this really rocks the boat at home. Many times, she wants out. The truth that the woman needs to see is that the louder the bark, the weaker the person. Just because he yells and has to have his own way, doesn't give him license to control you.

The Good Girls Who Always Want to Please

I want to please my husband so he won't leave me.
I do anything my boss asks to keep my job.

Many women who never really felt loved as little girls feel like they have to be really "good" to earn love. Their intimate relationships are therefore unbalanced or unequal. The women feel powerless and thus give their power away to their spouses or lovers. "He'll love me if I please him, do what he wants, say what he wants to hear, give in, let him win, or be right. If I don't please him, he may go away or hurt or yell at me. I better not rock the boat or confront a problem.

Many women traditionally have been passive not only in their general behavior, but also with their lovers. The self-defeating messages they hear in their heads are, "Let the man take the lead. Nice girls don't initiate lovemaking." They don't initiate love-play. Some fear causing resentment in their mate by initiating sexual overtures. Then at the other extreme, there are women who try so hard to please their partners that they engage in sexual acts at their lovers' demands.

Women as "Rescuers"

Stella's Story

I looked for a weaker man so I could feel more powerful, secure, and needed. My father was very domineering with my mother and finally left her.

*I didn't want to have to put up with what my
mother did, so I found an easygoing man I could
control. Tom was weaker and seemed appealing.
What I wanted was an "insurance policy"
against being left. I lied to myself by thinking
that "if I control him, he will never leave."
However, after a while, the relationship developed into one of parent–child. In the "parent"
role, I got frustrated and angry with Tom, lost
respect for him, became resentful, and no longer
enjoyed the relationship. I want a lover, a partner, not a child.*

Looking for a Man Like Dad

Some women idolize their fathers so much that
they seek men much like their dads. They may admire
particular characteristics in their fathers, such as
sensitivity, assertiveness, or an outgoing personality.
Looking for a guy just like dear old Dad isn't a
mistake. If you're lucky enough to have a Dad you
admire, find a man with Dad's characteristics.

Married to Cheaters

Some women are married to cheaters who seek
excitement outside the marriage. Some women don't
know this is happening, and some do. Knowing is a
downer. Doing something about it is a choice. With
self-esteem and power you recognize that you have
options, alternatives, and can take the actions you
choose.

Consider the options of "the other woman." If *She*
succeeds in getting your man away from you, chances
are that after a while he will seek another woman and
leave her in the position you may be in now.

Should you trust again? Should you go out on your
own? Can you do it alone? Many women say, "I have
no choice." The fearful woman who doubts herself
may say, "I can't. Who will take care of me. I better

stay and settle. Maybe he will change." Other confident women say, "I'll be okay. I have what it takes. I can make it on my own."

The Dating/Mating Game

There are different rules for the dating game as we approach the year 2000. Things are totally different from what they were in the 1960s and 1970s, and even the 1980s. For a long time, the common morality of American middle-class society said that sexual activity should be saved for marriage. We had a double standard. It was okay for boys but not for girls. Somehow young men always found willing partners. "Loose" women were scorned as tramps, while sexual conquests for boys were applauded.

Then came the sexual revolution, and couples experimented with sex as an early step in getting acquainted. Next came free and frequent sex with many partners, one-night stands, open marriages, and even partner exchanges. Then came herpes, and then the AIDS plague. There was a halt to casual sex and unprotected activity to guard against sexually transmitted diseases. With the advent of "safe sex" came the realization that sex should come after a development of a real relationship when two people agree and are careful.

Men "In the Candy Store": What Margie Says

I met a wonderful man. Joe was just a few months out of a divorce after a twenty-year marriage. We hit it off well. We had a lot in common, and it was easy to laugh together. It felt to me like the beginning of a nice relationship. Then he told me that he didn't want to see me more than once a week because he didn't want any commitment.

Margie is like many women who want a committed relationship, while men want their autonomy. Unfortunately for Margie, Joe was in a time of his life when he wanted to sample more of what he thought he had missed during marriage. Sometimes timing is everything. A year later, when Joe met Alice, he was ready to settle down—and he did, with Alice.

Even in this age of postponed marriage, many young women hear society's message that says: "You're not okay if you're not in a couple." Thus many single women ask themselves, "Am I defective" or "What's wrong with me?" Many women seek a committed relationship, while some men fear a loss of autonomy by committing themselves to one woman.

Many women are still single in their late 30s with few prospects of getting married. Some feel their "biological clocks" ticking. To satisfy their urge toward motherhood, some take in foster children. Others adopt as single parents. Some have a baby without a mate. Artificial insemination techniques make this possible; others recruit male friends to father their children. According to Pam Mohr of the American Bar Association's Center on Children and the Law: "These women do a lot of planning for their lives to accommodate the children. They are mature women and better able to handle motherhood than many very young, married women. They know it will be difficult to raise a child on their own, but they are prepared for it."

Single: Making the First Move

Some say that it is easier for a man to meet a woman than the other way around. Others think it is the men who do the "asking out." However, in today's society, a woman CAN call a man, and women do ask men out. Women of all ages have much less trouble making the first moves than women of older generations. Today it's acceptable for the woman to call the man, whether she's 16 or 66.

Marriage and Divorce: "What Did I Do Wrong?"

High divorce rates of the last few decades and women's low self-esteem seem to have run a parallel course. Many divorced women feel squashed when men abandon them for younger women. These women let themselves feel blame and guilt, and therefore defer too much to men. Many women who had great expectations from a relationship or from a marriage go unfulfilled. Many think a flawed relationship was their fault. Many lose self-esteem by feeling like the "guilty" party—or being made to feel so by their partner. They need boosters! One booster that suits these people is the realization that nice people can have irreconcilable differences. Nice people are lovable.

The changing gender roles of the 1990s have given women more equality with men in the workplace and home (with shared household and childcare responsibilities), causing some men to feel threatened. Conflicts over gender roles, for some couples, leads to conflict and ultimately divorce. Many women who might have been passive and subservient in previous decades now feel the freedom to express their interests and pursue their own goals. However, in some cases the solution is divorce, even after much counseling and soul-searching.

After Divorce: What Power, What Freedoms?

Divorced women face a separate set of power and self-esteem issues, such as society's opinion that a woman without a man is a lesser being, that she is a "fifth wheel" at a dinner party, that because she is out of a marriage (even if it was her choice) she may be somewhat less lovable. She faces questions from friends (particularly married men) about why she hasn't remarried, why she doesn't meet more men. All of these issues may cause the woman to have even more self-doubts.

Divorce Can Affect Children

Some girls who grow up in single-parent homes develop ideas that lead to difficulties in developing successful intimate relationships later on. However, with the Womanpower Boosting Cycle, even lifelong patterns can be overcome. Here's Irene:

I'm 37. Mom and Dad divorced when I was 13. He was very domineering. He expected me to be "perfect." I guess he expected Mom to be, too. He really turned Mom against men. Dad remarried, but Mom, now 64, never remarried, although she passed over several opportunities. For a long time, I was afraid I would never get married and would be alone, just like Mom. When I dated in high school and college, I always picked men who were not like my father. I saw what having a domineering mate did to my mother, and to their marriage. So I picked guys who didn't expect me to be perfect and who were not controlling people. Looking back, they were what we think of as "wimps," and I got bored with them. Then I would meet another guy and repeat the pattern all over again. With therapy, I realized what I was doing. I knew that I could take care of myself. I didn't need a guy to take care of me. I had a good education and a good job. I came to see that while at first I was attracted to the wimpy personalities unlike Dad, after a while I was put off by the guys who couldn't take care of themselves. Now I've met a wonderful man who can take care of himself very well. Like me, he also

*wants closeness. We accept each other as whole
selves. We don't expect each other to be perfect. I
think we have a Type D relationship. That's the
kind of relationship that is Me, You, and Us (1 +
1 + 1 = 3). There is equal sharing, and no one
gives up any of himself or herself. We each have
brought a lot to it. We are each growing individu-
ally and our relationship is growing.*

Relationships Change: When Baby Makes Three

Some young couples with troubled relationships
think that having a baby will improve the situation.
"If we have a child, it will fix things." Usually this
isn't the case. Here's Sleepless Sandy:

*We were so happy when Danny arrived. But it put
a strain on our relationship. We never got enough
sleep, we had less time alone together, less time
for making love. My husband, Jon, seemed to feel
left out and a little jealous. I had to quit my job,
and we had less money with the additional responsibility. We started having arguments that
we never had before. Jon had a fear of being a
parent, and thought that he wouldn't be able to
live up to my expectations. He remembered
things from his own childhood that got in his way
of being a good parent himself. At the same time,
I was feeing really down, probably as a result of
hormonal changes right after childbirth. All these
things really stressed our marriage, close to the
breaking point.*

According to Dale S. Gody, Ph.D., a psychotherapist in Wilmette, Illinois, marriage is never the same
after the arrival of a baby. Before the baby, Sandy and
Jon had developed conscious or unconscious rules
about their degree of closeness and distance, intimacy
and autonomy, as well as tolerance for conflict and

anger. When little Danny came, the old balance was challenged. Conflicts in what had been a close relationship occurred for the first time.

Improving Communication after Baby's Arrival

Sandy and Jon quickly became aware of what they were doing to each other and their relationship. After very short-term psychotherapy as a couple, here's what they learned:

> We started talking about expectations of ourselves regarding childcare and household responsibilities. That's something we should have considered even before Danny arrived. We learned to communicate our own needs and feelings with "I" statements. We learned to avoid assumptions, accusations, and blame, which usually start with "You." We found ways to resume some things we enjoyed doing together. Because we didn't have any grandmothers around, we began to ask friends, or hire a sitter so we could go out with each other and not always take Danny. We also learned to negotiate. For example, I do the dishes if Jon agrees to give Danny his bath. Or I get up with the baby one night, if Jon will do the same for me the next night.

Sandy and Jon, like many couples, were each able to preserve and enhance their sense of self. Neither felt they were giving up anything for their relationship as a threesome. Their relationship is again a Type D, and with Danny, a D+. Couples with or without children, or roommates who share space and chores, can adapt these techniques for compromise.

Start Improving Your Relationships Today

I always say yes to my girlfriend. She's prettier than I am and has more friends. If I don't do what she wants, she won't want me around.

I'm the one who gets stuck with cleaning up after a party. I don't ask my roommate to help because she pays more rent than I do.

I'd better have sex when he wants, even if I'm not in the mood.

I better not initiate sex; I don't want him to think I'm too forward.

Sound familiar? If this is you, chances are you are still suppressing yourself, pleasing your partner or friend, and feeling very frustrated. You can't possibly feel very good about yourself or enjoy your intimate relationship if you are *always* putting the other person first and pleasing them instead of yourself. Be more assertive. You will feel better!

Look back at Chapter 3. Consider what your "stuck spots" are. Have you identified them? What areas of your relationship would you like to change? How hard are you trying to get yourself "unstuck"? List the areas of your life you want to change. What is in the way? From what past experiences do your self-defeating messages come?

Feeling loved, needed, and wanted are the biggest boosts women can have. Look at the list of Personal Rights in Chapter 3 (pages 77–78). Think about how you can integrate permission, freedom, choice, options, risk, action, power and self-esteem into your life. Consider your alternatives. Start your action plan now. Move forward in love and friendship. You can do it!

7

GET YOURSELF AND
YOUR CAREER ON TRACK

What *did* you want to be when you were a little girl? Have you reached those goals? Are you still trying? Have you redefined your goals as the years rolled by? If you're lucky, you feel satisfied with where you are in your career. If not, perhaps it's time for another look at why you aren't satisfied and how you might give yourself a boost.

〰〰〰〰〰〰〰〰〰〰〰〰〰〰〰〰〰〰

JOBPOWER

Jobpower is part of Womanpower. Jobpower is being satisfied with the work you've chosen, and feeling professionally fulfilled, appreciated, and recognized for your abilities. It is feeling competent in your skills and getting promotions you deserve. It is also a willingness to speak up to your boss and co-workers when necessary. Where do you stand on the Jobpower scale?

Here's a quiz to help you determine if you are as powerful as you can and want to be in the workplace. If you answer YES to most of the questions, you probably have developed a good sense of Womanpower. If you answer NO to most of the questions, your Jobpower needs a boost.

THE JOBPOWER SCALE

	YES	NO
Are you satisfied with your job?		
Do you feel professionally fulfilled?		
Do you feel you are using your talents and skills?		
Are you appreciated at work and recognized for your accomplishments?		
Are you in a field you like?		
Do others respect you on your job?		
Do you feel secure and confident on your job?		
Do you feel competent to do the work you do?		
Are you paid according to your ability?		
Are you getting promotions you deserve?		
Are you happy going to work most of the time?		
Do you feel you have equality with men at your workplace?		
Is your salary comparable to men's for the same job?		

	YES	NO
Do you get the advancements that men get?		
Do men respect you for your professionalism?		
Are you willing to go the "extra mile" to help others in your workplace?		
Can you appreciate others' successes at work?		
Are you able to speak up to your boss and co-workers?		
Are you really interested in the work you do?		

If you said NO to many of the above questions, you may be stuck in a situation from which you would like to emerge. You may have your eye on another job but feel stuck in getting going toward it. Apply the material you have read in earlier chapters to your job situation. Remember the chapter about finding your "stuck spots"? How hard are you trying to make changes? How committed are you to making changes? Nothing will happen unless you make it happen. Let the Womanpower Boosting Cycle help you. Go through the four "A" steps again: Apply them to your personal situation now.

Awareness
Acceptance
Alternatives
Action

What's Holding You Back?

Although gender bias still exists, it seems like a poor excuse for most women not getting ahead. Women ARE powerful. Remember our female ancestors who crossed the country in covered wagons? Or those who were the only women in their professional schools? Those women were powerful and brave. They had to be. They had strength and self-esteem.

Today women need many strengths, perhaps even more than in previous generations. Women who work also need power to balance home life, families, and careers successfully. Women want to be powerful and confident yet remain feminine. With Womanpower, they can feel and project self-confidence on the job as well as in their personal relationships.

Generational Differences in Career Paths

Pamela A. Mohr, former executive director for the Alliance for Children's Rights, Los Angeles, and now with the Center on Children and the Law is a third-generation female lawyer. Her mother and grandmother were lawyers who graduated from the University of Chicago School of Law. Her grandmother was the only woman in her class and went on to become a founder of the Chicago chapter of the American Civil Liberties Union. Pam's mother and father met in law school. Her mother was one of three women in the class and practiced law for a year until Pam was born. To indicate how times have changed, in Pam's law school class (1984) at UCLA—the University of California, Los Angeles—35 percent of the graduates were women. In 1995, the number of female graduates has climbed to 45 percent of the class.

Gender Bias: As the Twentieth Century Ends

We've all encountered gender bias in the workplace at some time. However, today, because of legislation and the emergence of many assertive women there is less gender bias than ever before, but it is still there. Pam Mohr was in private law practice before founding the Alliance. Here's what Pam says:

> *There were times when I went to depositions and the other lawyers assumed I was a court reporter, not a lawyer. My worst day was in a heated court hearing when a male judge said something to me that sounded like, "Calm down, little girl." It was hard to know what to say. I didn't want to hurt my case, but I couldn't let his remark go unanswered. I said: "Your Honor, I've been practicing law for five years. I appreciate your comment on my youthfulness. I'd like to go on with the argument."*

We admire Pamela's Womanpower! How we wish we could think that fast and respond with an appropriately professional comeback!

Gender Bias a Generation Ago

Here's what Ada experienced on her first job:

> *It was during the late 1950s, in my very first job out of college. A female editor hired me as assistant editor. We were a two-person staff. Before she introduced me to the top boss, the publisher, I overheard him say to her, "She's pretty, but does she know production?" I was flattered, a little embarrassed, and knew that I had to prove to him through good work that thanks to my training in journalism school, indeed I did know how to produce a magazine!*
>
> *Another time, I interviewed for a position as editor of* Recreation Management, *a magazine about industrial recreation. I was rejected. "We want a man in the editor job. But you can freelance for us." In the course of the next*

several years, I sold more than thirty articles to that publication."

Pat's Story: Letter to Her Teacher

I'm 31 and an attorney. I was a slow learner in high school. In my first year, a teacher advised me against going into education, or even trying to complete four years of college because I read slower than my classmates. I always took longer to do assignments. In my second year, an English teacher determined that I had dyslexia—which was the cause of my slow reading. With special help, I boosted my reading ability and self-esteem. I finished high school, got into a good college and then completed law school.

Recently, Pat wrote a long letter to her high-school teacher. She told of her achievements and pleaded with that teacher to never again squash a student's enthusiasm for learning and career goals.

Deferring to Men and Other Power Drains

What do you do when you are with a group of male associates? Do you speak up? Do you hold back your ideas? Are you assertive? Do you utilize the skills you learned in Chapter 4?

Some women have not developed the self-esteem and confidence to trust and express their own ideas. Sandra, a 39-year-old corporate executive, usually begins her statements in meetings with male executives with "What would you think if . . ." Often the men on the management committee like her ideas, but instead of saying so and praising her, they put her down. Then they present the same ideas as their own. If Sandra would become more assertive and learn to say, for example, "This is the action I recommend . . ." the men would be less likely to put her ideas down and reconstruct them as their own.

Here are some examples of statements many women make that put them in the "power drain" mode instead of on the Womanpower track:

POWER DRAIN	WOMANPOWER TRACK
What would you think if I suggested buying an additional piece of property for a parking lot?	We should buy property adjacent to our new lot and get a parking lot up and running.
This may sound like a dumb question, but why can't we hire a temporary clerk while I'm on vacation?	Hiring a temporary clerk while I'm on vacation would really keep this project rolling along on schedule.
I know you're not interested, but here's something you ought to know about.	ABC company has just hired a management consultant to do what our committee is trying to do.

You're getting the idea, right? Say what you have to say. Don't back into your statement with a weak beginning. You will be taken more seriously if you present your idea with confidence and assertiveness. Tell yourself, "What I have to say is important, has value and is worth being heard." Women who hold back their own ideas may have grown up with the notion that boys will not like them if there are too smart. When these women go to work, they find it hard to present themselves as equals with the men in business. Here's Rosie, an example of a young woman who admits to all this:

In school I was smart. I didn't even have to study very much to get top grades. When I started getting the best grade in the room, I started screwing up on tests. I wanted to be one of the kids. I thought I would be treated like an outcast if I was smarter than the boys. I got mediocre grades by trying to make mistakes. Now it's hard for me to present myself on an equal footing with the men in the office, but I'm working on it.

Be Taken More Seriously

The AAUW study in 1990 reported that for elementary-school girls, academic confidence is the most important aspect of self-esteem, yet for them it is already a negative force. Less than 49 percent of the girls in elementary school said they felt pride in their schoolwork, and that percentage dropped to 12 percent in high school. (Academic pride plays a smaller role in the structure of boys' self-esteem.)

The AAUW study also found a strong relationship between math and science and adolescent self-esteem. Math and science have the strongest relationship to self-esteem for young women, and as they "learn" that they are not good at these topics, their sense of self-worth and aspiration diminish.

When young women grow up with squashed self-esteem, it carries over into professional life. Some women in professional fields have gone from squashed self-esteem and non-assertiveness to passivity. Being non-assertive makes one passive and invisible in terms of getting credit and moving upward.

Some women in professional situations believe the only way to be recognized and taken seriously is to be like a man and act harsh and tough. Consider the case of the woman who is so tough at work that her colleagues call her "the bitch on wheels." Aggressiveness may give her short-term power, but eventually, toughness works against her.

Womanpower Combines Capability and Smiles

Women don't have to be like men to be successful. Women can be feminine and still exude confidence. Women can wear dresses in the office; they don't have to always wear tailored suits. Women can let men open car doors and help them on with their coats. Letting men be helpful doesn't undermine your power. If a man calls you "honey" or "sweetheart," accept it as a term of personal endearment, not a put-down. You can call him "honey," too.

Believe it or not, smiling can help you get ahead. According to a study presented at the 1993 meeting of the American Association for the Advancement of Science, smiling can help you get ahead on the job. Don't let your problems show on your face at work. Smile and the world will smile back.

At the meeting, Linda Carli, a psychologist from Wellesley College, presented studies that suggested that working women who are merely competent do not succeed as well as those who also appear warm and likable to male colleagues. She found that in tests, males presented with the same message were more receptive when a female speaker appeared friendly, smiled, and leaned toward the audience. "When it comes to influencing a man, it seems that women must be more than competent. They must get their point across with warmth."

What About the "Glass Ceiling"?

Today's professional women are still bumping up against invisible barriers while climbing the corporate ladder: the glass ceiling. The "glass ceiling" is an impenetrable barrier perceived by working women, one they believe keeps them from rising to the top of their field, despite their good qualifications, experience, and hard work. Estimates of women in top management positions in the mid-1980s range from 2 to 4 percent in spite of the fact that college enrollment is more than 50 percent women, and women make up about one quarter of the enrollment in Master of Business Administration (MBA) programs.

The glass ceiling may take many forms. Men may be brought into high-level positions in the organization from outside, in the name of providing a fresh outlook and new blood, while the qualified women already in the organization are passed over. In some organizations involving teamwork and negotiations, discussions may be held in such a way that women are kept on the periphery. Women in lower-level positions are sometimes given responsible, demanding work, which is not compensated. As women attempt to make progress in an organization, they may be frustrated by performance standards that are higher for them than for men. Women may also be limited by assumptions that there is a feminine management style that is more passive and nurturing toward fellow workers and less goal-oriented and driven than the masculine style.

Women who do make it past the glass ceiling frequently credit the influence of a mentor, spouse, or parent. Some women have decided to avoid the glass ceiling by striking out on their own. In the late 1980s and after, the number of successful self-employed women increased faster than men. Two well-known successes are Liz Claiborne and Mrs. Fields Cookies.

A 1992 survey of women CPAs by the American Woman's Society of Certified Public Accountants (AWSCPA) found that more than half (55 percent) of those responding had left a job because they had reached a glass ceiling. Additionally, 67 percent said they would look for a job in another organization if they thought a glass ceiling was preventing them from reaching their career goal.

"Eliminating the glass ceiling is one of the most important remodeling projects now facing American business," says Joyce Simon, past-president of AWSCPA and a former partner in a major accounting firm. "Women at any job level need to act now to take control of their careers and to plan, execute, and evaluate their career paths."

In the AWSCPA survey, 25 percent believed they had reached a glass ceiling in their present job, while 45 percent believed other women in their firms had reached a glass ceiling. In that survey, half (48 percent) believed they did not receive the same opportunities as male colleagues, while 43 percent disagreed. Simon offers a strategic outline for career planning and control, including developing a vision, identifying milestones, taking charge, selecting a mentor, and using informal networks.

"Working harder and smarter is only part of our current situation. You have to plan your career path and adjust your vision regularly as your dreams and reality change," she says.

Dealing with Sexual Harassment

In school and at work, women often have to handle the issue of sexual harassment. Sexual harassment means unwanted and uninvited sexual attentions, whether from men toward women, women toward men, or toward same-sex individuals. Such attentions may include jokes and remarks, questions about the other's sexual behavior, "accidental" touching, and repeated and unwanted invitations for a date or a sexual relationship. Sexual harassment is aggressive behavior because it tends to "put down" the victim and make the violator feel more powerful. He (or she) wants to "depower" you by making remarks or innuendos.

It is only in the last two decades that the issue of sexual harassment has come out into the open. For example, in 1980, a U.S. Supreme Court decision (Meritor v. Vinson) declared that sexual harassment is a form of sex discrimination and, therefore, a violation of Title VII of the 1964 Civil Rights Act. In

1991, sexual harassment received national attention when a female lawyer accused a nominee for the U.S. Supreme Court of sexual harassment and the federal hearing was nationally televised. What can women do to avoid or counter sexual harassment in school or at work?

- File a complaint with the personnel director
- Tell the offender to stop
- Avoid the person(s)
- Tell a superior

Under federal law, it is the responsibility of management to ensure a workplace that employees feel is fair, with equal opportunity for all. According to Carol Kleiman, columnist for the *Chicago Tribune,* the best deterrent to harassment is a working atmosphere that says everyone is equal.

In Pamela Mohr's previous work with the Alliance for Children's Rights, she frequently encountered cases involving junior-high and high-school girls who had been subjected to inappropriate comments and even touching. "This is harassment. Girls need to learn to speak up. That's the way it can be stopped in this generation. We help girls determine what remedies are available to them."

Maximize Your Power:
Set Priorities and Meet Deadlines

The best way to compete successfully in what you might perceive as "a man's world" is to do the best possible job. A good start toward giving yourself a boost at work is to feel that you are keeping up with what you have to do. Gain control over your time by making a few changes in your style of working. For example, you can sort your priorities by deadlines. Some deadlines are real and others are more flexible.

Delegate work and responsibility whenever appropriate. Trust others to do tasks that will free up your time for your high-priority tasks. When really pushed for time, keep your cool and stay in control of the situation.

HOW PRODUCTIVE ARE YOU?

Some women are slow to get going and slow to get things done; other, more productive, women seem to whiz through paperwork. They keep things organized. They get along well with their supervisors, peers, and, employees. They know how and are able to delegate. If you say YES to most of the following, you need to take a close look at your working habits and try to improve your skills.

MOST OF THE TIME THE FOLLOWING TERMS SOUND LIKE ME:	YES	NO
Lack of organization		
Misplaced items		
Procrastination		
Perfectionism		
Do not use a team approach		
Difficulty listening		
Inability to say NO		
Not trusted by others		
Do not trust others		
Do not confront problems		
Avoid difficult situations		
Do not stand up for your rights		

	YES	NO
Unnecessary correspondence		
Act indecisively		
Do not praise others for good work		
Lack of confidence in difficult situations		
Do not consider "political" agendas of others		
Not connected (networked) to the right people		

If you said YES to most of these questions, your assertiveness probably needs a boost. For example, if you believe that you communicate poorly with others, are not comfortable showing your authority, have an inability to say NO, are indecisive and lack confidence, your assertiveness can be improved. You may want to reread Chapter 4.

You can also use the Womanpower Boosting Cycle to determine your stuck spots. Are you aware of what your problems are? Do you acknowledge and take responsibility for these situations? What alternatives can you consider in dealing with your day-to-day situations? What action can you take to become more productive? You are in control of your time. Make the most of it.

Making Presentations: A "Stuck Spot" for Many

In school or at work, you may be called upon to make a presentation, give a talk, or stand up in front of a committee to make a report. Some women avoid

speaking in front of an audience. This is a very
common fear, but women who have overcome it feel
more powerful and confident. Women who can make
an effective presentation gain respect and authority in
their school or organization.

If you are in the "fearful group," once you get past
the anxiety of speaking in front of others, which is
a very common fear, you will feel more confident.
Consider what makes you fearful. Were you ever
embarrassed when speaking in front of people? Are
you giving yourself "rubber-band" bounce-back,
self-defeating messages? If you're thinking, "They
will laugh at me, I'll mess up, they won't like me,"
change your self-defeating squashers to boosters.
Think of times you have successfully given talks or
spoken up. Change your squashers to boosters, for
example:

"I can do this. I've done it before. They liked my
talk."

"I'm prepared and I know my material."

"I make a good appearance. I speak with authority."

"I have a lot of interesting things to say."

"People will like me and my speaking style."

Here are a few helpful tips that can give you
Womanpower before making a presentation:

- Do your "homework" before the meeting and
  learn something about your audience. Are they
  men, women, or a mixed audience? What are
  their backgrounds?
- Practice your talk in front of a friend. Ask for
  and accept feedback.
- Practice relaxation techniques that will help
  you get over your initial nervousness or anxiety.

- Join Toastmasters, a club which fosters confidence and ability for public speaking. Look in your local yellow pages for details. This club can help you improve your speaking techniques and help you feel more comfortable in front of an audience.
- Keep an outline on small cards in front of you.
- Accept the fact that you feel fearful; go ahead anyway.
- Try to keep your audience involved; let them interact.
- Consider difficult questions your audience might ask that would throw you off guard
- Plan ahead to answer some of the objections your audience may raise to points in your report or presentation.
- Prepare an attention-getting summary of your talk.

Practice makes perfect. If you feel fearful about speaking in front of others, start by giving a talk before what you regard as a "low-threat" audience. This may be a church group or a group of people you know well. Later you can progress to work in more public situations.

Mismatches Are Power Drains

Ways to boost self-esteem on the job include choosing a career track that fits you, your interests, your capabilities, and your aspirations. Mismatched situations can't boost your self-esteem. Choose carefully. At a recent seminar on self-esteem, which Sheila presented, Janet, a 57-year-old executive secretary, spoke of her experience. Janet had worked twenty years for a company that went out of business when its founder died. Within a month, she found a new job. She had been working for three months, but she

found that she just couldn't keep up with the pace of
the busy construction office and wasn't familiar with
the terminology or forms used.

> *My self-esteem was low. The people in this office
> made me feel like I didn't know anything. I felt
> devastated and afraid to leave and get another
> job. Sheila suggested that I acknowledge that this
> new job is a "mismatch" and no reflection on my
> twenty years of good work and accomplishments.
> With this thought as a booster, I will leave this
> job and look for another, with confidence in
> myself.*

Hearing about Janet reminded Ada of an experience she had when she took a new position after
having gained a reputation as a successful medical
writer. The job was with a leading public-relations
agency. This situation turned out to be a complete
mismatch.

> *Although I went in at a very high executive level, I
> had expectations of having training and support
> staff that the agency didn't meet. And the agency
> had expectations that I didn't meet. After six
> weeks, this was apparent to both sides. I knew the
> situation had to be terminated. My choices:*

POOR CHOICES	BETTER CHOICES
Feel devastated	Swallow pride (I don't belong here)
Feel degraded	Leave gracefully

> *I acknowledged to myself and the vice president
> that I didn't belong there. The VP said he ad-
> mired me for leaving so gracefully. I left, self-
> esteem intact. And, as they say, the rest is history.
> I moved on to establish a women's health pro-*

gram that in six years became the leader in its area.

Sheila's Turning Point

Some women let "mismatched" job situations devastate them. They can be overwhelmed. Women with self-esteem use their power to make the bad situation a turning point toward opening new doors. Sheila had worked her way up to be principal of a school for mentally retarded and emotionally disturbed children, but she wasn't happy.

> *I was unhappy because I wasn't in direct contact with the kids. I was a trained counselor working as an administrator. I wanted to quit but was afraid to. I wanted to become a private psychotherapist and see individuals on a one-to-one basis. I wondered, Who will hire me? Who will come to me for therapy? Before I quit the job, I got a part-time job at a local community college adult-education program, teaching "Psychology of Personal Growth" and hung out my private-therapy shingle. I did my psychotherapy from 4–9 P.M. and still had the job in the school. I proved that I could teach and get private clients. Finally I got the courage to turn in my letter of resignation to the college.*

Find Womanpower, Find Satisfaction

We all have down days at work once in a while. But women with Womanpower generally feel satisfied with their pathway and also have a feeling of high self-esteem. For many women, satisfaction on the job means that they feel a reasonable degree of contentment, feel in control of their situation, and enjoy their work. These women have the skills necessary to do their work and also feel a sense of challenge from their career.

On the other hand, women who feel that there is a great deal of challenge and they are not prepared with appropriate skills, experience stress and anxiety on the job. Those who have a high level of skill and do not feel challenged become frustrated and have difficulty being motivated. Those who are not skilled and have no challenge develop a feeling of boredom and frustration. Those with low self-esteem doubt their abilities to achieve, so they keep themselves in lower-level, less-satisfying jobs because of fear of failure. Some fear success and tell themselves, "I'm not worthy."

If you have family responsibilities and a job, accept the fact that it is likely that you will be the one who gets the brunt of crisis situations, not your husband. Pamela Mohr says this: "I've watched many husbands and wives who are both partners in law firms. When their children or elderly parents are sick, it is usually the woman who takes care of the dependent—and without resentment. Perhaps we have the maternal instinct, or maybe it is something we were taught as girls. For single women who adopt children, this is also true.

At a meeting recently, we heard about a self-esteem survey in which women who worked part-time were compared with women who worked full-time. Surprisingly, or maybe not so surprisingly, women who worked part-time felt a higher sense of self-esteem. Why? The full-time working mothers evaluated themselves on a number of roles—wife, mother, and professional. All the roles are demanding of time, attention, and competence. "I compete with men in the office who don't have the responsibilities I have at home," said one. Most of the part-timers, however, felt that they were performing well at their job and at home, and had greater satisfaction, thereby boosting their self-esteem.

Take Control of Your Career or Career Plans

Joyce Simon, past president of the women's CPA society (AWSCPA), says, "Treat your career like a business. Prepare a strategic plan, and after executing your plan, find a way to evaluate your results." Here are six basic steps to take control:

1. Develop your vision. What type of position do you want to achieve? When? Where do you want to be in five years? What types of environments are you happiest in? What kinds of tasks are you happiest doing? Be a dreamer, but be realistic at the same time. Understand your strengths and weaknesses. Understand the competition. Who are they? What are they like? What types of skills will you need to get ahead in the field or company you have chosen? What level of performance will you have to achieve to be successful?

2. Prepare your action plan. Prepare yourself. Consider short- and long-range goals. Include continuing-education plans as well as self-improvement plans. You need to have the right skills and the right appearance to meet your plan's goals.

3. Make a commitment to your success. Always keep your vision in mind. Remember, you are the most important person who can make your job or career work.

4. Seek opportunities and challenges. Take the initiative. Ask for what you want. Don't keep your creativity to yourself. Make suggestions. Offer to take the lead in implementing your own suggestions. Demonstrate your commitment to your employer. Take advantage of opportunities to expand your own skills.

5. Become involved in more than your job. Outside activities help you balance your life,

expand your horizons, and provide opportunities to further your leadership and organizational skills.

6. Network. Never eat lunch alone. Invite a coworker. If you are reluctant to ask a man out to lunch, ask two men, and you will be a group. Be your own public relations manager. Toot your own horn. Let others know about your capabilities, accomplishments, and dreams.

Put It All Together: Get the Boost You Need

Womanpower on the job means having goals, directing your energy toward those goals, and moving ahead. It is satisfaction with what you are doing. It is feeling good about yourself. For married women or mothers who work, it may mean carefully balancing home and work. It may mean balancing the needs of marriage (and children or elderly parents) with the needs of the job. Try not to have unrealistic expectations of yourself. Give yourself permission not to be The Superwoman: don't expect yourself to be "the perfect Mom" as well as perfect in your job. Don't push yourself into a corner; that's a sure way to feel overwhelmed and frustrated.

Linda Hughey Holt, M.D., a suburban Chicago-area obstetrician-gynecologist and mother of three young children, says, "Being a working Mom is a constant juggling act. We have lots of balls in the air at once. Sometimes one of them falls. So what? Let it fall. You don't have to be perfect."

Whatever your situation, use the techniques you have read about in this book. You may want to look back at the chapters on the four "A" steps to get yourself going toward Womanpower. At every turn on your career track, develop Awareness of your situation. Accept responsibility for your choices. Decide to make changes. Learn about new choices. Gather your data. Develop some Alternatives if you feel stuck. Then take Action. Move forward!

8

UNBURDEN YOUR SECRET: GAIN MORE PERSONAL POWER

Keeping a secret is a heavy burden that can squash your self-esteem. Keeping secrets may mean that you are listening to old negative self-talk messages that keep bouncing back to haunt you and probably hurt your mental and physical wellness. This chapter will help you use the four "A" steps in additional ways to boost your self-esteem and also help you realize that you have a choice regarding keeping secrets.

Human Nature: Keeping Secrets

If you have a secret that you are hiding, you are not alone. If you have a secret you've not told anyone, you aren't any different than the people around you. Look around you in a crowded restaurant, train station, church service, or while walking down a city street. Many people have secrets haunting them. There may be some who were married once and never told their second spouse. Some may currently be victims of abuse by their husbands or wives. There may be men and women who want to keep their sexual orientation a secret, women who are secret alcoholics and agoraphobics and are afraid to venture out of their homes without a trusted person. There may be women who had abortions or gave babies away, people who know they are adopted and never even told their spouses. Some may have committed a crime. Others may have a history of mental illness in their family or once attempted suicide. All these secrets are burdens.

To overcome your unwanted feelings of powerlessless and low self-esteem, which may have resulted from keeping a secret, you can follow the Womanpower Boosting Cycle by using the four "A" steps described in an earlier chapter:

- Awareness
- Acceptance
- Alternatives
- Action

Throughout *Empower Yourself,* you've read details about how this plan can help you boost your power and self-esteem. Now you can use the same Womanpower Boosting Cycle to relieve the hurting and haunting you suffer because of your secret.

Why Secrets Hold You Back

The word "secret" comes from the Latin word *secretus,* meaning "separate" or "out of the way." The current definition, according to the *American Heritage Dictionary of the English Language,* includes the following:

- Something kept hidden from others or known only to oneself or to a few
- Concealed from general knowledge or view
- Dependably closemouthed; discreet
- Not visibly expressed; private; inward

The definition implies a holding back, holding within, rather than being outgoing and moving forward. With the four "A" steps, you can learn to let go of the secret and move forward. Once you have taken the step of *Awareness* and know that your secret is a burden, and the step of *Acceptance,* which means knowing that only you can make changes, you're ready to consider *Alternatives* and *Action.*

Awareness: Your Secret vs. Your Self-Esteem

Part of the process of letting go of a secret involves working through the secret from the past and coming to terms with it. What's your secret? What are you hiding? What are you afraid to tell? Did something happen in your past that you hope no one ever finds out?

You *can* let go. You can work through the haunting painful messages of the past. The first step toward letting go is to be **aware** how keeping a secret affects you and your self-esteem. Once this becomes clear to you, use some personally tailored boosters. You may have to go back into your past, replaying a life event that caused your pain. You'll have to deal with the pain, confront it, and bring your new thinking up to the present. You will be able to let go of the stigma, pain, and the part of the secret you use against yourself to squash your self-esteem.

Acceptance: Why Keeping a Secret Takes Energy

You are now ready to accept the fact that it takes energy worrying about keeping a secret. We feel scared, threatened, and held back from letting our real selves emerge. Many of us struggle lifelong with the secrets we keep. Some of us think that there is something wrong in having a secret, but we don't know what to do about it. Some of us even think there is something wrong with us, and this thought alone makes us feel powerless in many areas of our lives.

Secrets get in the way of empowerment and boosted self-esteem. Some secrets become all-consuming. Some of us have serious secrets, such as having committed a crime. Others have less serious secrets, such as having had a nose straightened as a teenager; and an increasing number of women—and men— have undergone cosmetic surgery to change a body part. Then there are those who never tell their war-time secrets; those who undergo rigorous religious training for the priesthood or rabbinate and later lead a layman's life; or those in professional capacities, such as doctors or lawyers, who hide just as many secrets about themselves as the rest of us.

Hiding a non-visible disability, such as a vision or hearing impairment, or a disease such as diabetes or cancer, produces stresses that in turn may lead to other physical problems. Just as the size of ears and noses vary between individuals, so do the sizes and shapes of secrets vary between individuals. But the common factor among them is the resultant indecision, anxiety, and reduction of self-esteem they produce.

Physical Effects of Secrets vs. Self-Esteem

To tell or not to tell? As we continue to worry about hiding our secret, the stress produced by the hiding leads to body tension, resulting in psychophysiological (mind/body) illnesses such as headaches and stomachaches; behavioral symptoms, such as irritability, "short-fuse," and limited concentration; and psychological reactions, such as anxieties, depression and frustration.

Anxiety disorders are the number one mental health problem in the U.S.A. More than 16 million adults suffer from an anxiety disorder. Of those, about 10 million have depressive disorders. Compare that with the 6 1/2 million who have diabetes or the

2 million who have epilepsy. Of those who have anxiety disorders, an uncounted number may be made anxious by keeping secrets. It is not the secret itself that produces the anxiety, but rather what we do or don't do with it and how it affects our lives.

Alternatives: Deciding When to Tell

For some secrets, whether to tell or not is debatable. Some secrets should be told while others should not. Sort out your secrets and make your choices. Break free from the squashing grip your secret holds on you. The four "A" steps can help you understand the impact your secret has on your life, and if it's hurting you, how you can work through your pain and fear and then on to your choice of tell or don't tell.

Perhaps some secrets should be kept. Divulging some secrets at the wrong time to the wrong people CAN be embarrassing, shameful, and may interfere with one's life and lifestyle.

Many people keep their secrets because they are afraid of the repercussions if they tell. They believe that their self-esteem will diminish if others know what they know about themselves. Some fears ARE legitimate. Look at Ralph, a franchise restaurant manager who had just been diagnosed HIV-positive. He wondered if he should tell his new district manager. Unfortunately, in our society at this time, many people fear allowing anyone with this disease to handle food. Ralph came to the conscious, comfortable choice not to tell anyone, as long as he is feeling well and doing his job well.

On the other hand, telling a secret at an appropriate time to an appropriate person, may help you feel freer, unburdened, and enable you to let go of the fears that have been in your way. Telling can be a positive force and work to your benefit.

Sheila let go of her secret about her blindness after years of hiding. When Sheila was a teenager and began to date, she put a great deal of energy into hiding her disability. Once she had a date with a young man and attended a foreign film with subtitles. She couldn't see the subtitles at all, but never told. "He might not date me anymore if he finds out that I can't see," she thought.

During the 1970s, Sheila went through her own four "A" process and replaced the "Don't tell" message with "Tell if necessary." Now, having worked over the stigma of her secret, she simply tells audiences, "I can't see your hands when you raise them to ask questions. Just shout out your questions and I'll respond."

> *I worked through the message from my mother. I pretended to confront my mother. "Mom, you were wrong. I need to tell, otherwise people don't understand me—why I can't drive a car, and why I don't call on them when they raise their hands." This was all part of the four "A" steps. I had adopted my mother's incorrect assumption about society. I changed that assumption.*
>
> *Now I'm proud of my accomplishments. Telling is really no big deal, nothing as awful as what I imagined. I don't have to work hard anymore at hiding. Once I tell, I take energy away from hiding the secret and put the energy into getting on with my life.'*

That's why Sheila relates to the agonizing others go through regarding self-esteem and secrets. Her own experience helped lead toward the development of the Womanpower Boosting Cycle.

Another Alternative: Secrets to Divide and Share

Secrets can be divided into those to keep, those to let go of, and those to share. To boost your feelings of power and self-esteem, divide your secrets. Many couples share secrets—the intimacies of their relationship. Business associates share secrets. Mothers and daughters, fathers and sons share secrets. Many admit to shared secrets. One of our friends, Mary T. says she and her adult daughter share many secrets (even from their husbands), and that their sharing has reinforced their bond, their loving and supportive relationship. Fortunately for them, their shared secrets are "constructive" secrets.

Another friend, Melinda S., said that she felt complimented when her husband told her his lifelong secret about being adopted. "His telling me showed me that he trusted me," she said. This too, was a constructive, shared secret.

Can sharing a secret help a person overcome the burden of a perceived "destructive secret" that squashes self-esteem? The answer is often yes. Sandra found out, after months of inner turmoil and self-doubt. Sandra was called to Dallas from Topeka when her 25-year-old son, Don, was picked up by police for stealing a car. Don, a CPA, recently employed by a major accounting firm, outwardly appeared highly professional and ethical. After release following arrest, he admitted to his mother that he occasionally felt a compulsion to steal cars and had done so at least a dozen times since high school—"just for a lark"— but was never caught. Sandra went back to Topeka and her second husband. She felt ashamed of Don's predicament and told no one of her reason for flying to Dallas to visit Don. Over the next few months, while Don was awaiting trial, Sandra developed insomnia, became irritable, and frequently argued with her husband. Somehow she blamed herself for what had happened. Finally she went to a psychologist to talk about her own feeling of diminished self-esteem. She told her secret about her son. The psychologist said: "You didn't really need me. You just needed to tell someone."

Telling someone can be an *Action* step in some cases.

Shame vs. Self-Esteem

Some people are ashamed of their secret. That shame turns into feelings of powerlessness, low self-esteem, and possibly destructive, unwanted behaviors. There's Clara, who as a young teenager was smaller than other girls her age; she also had very bad acne. She was constantly teased and even hit several times because she wouldn't fight back when taunted by her peers. She never told her mother how the children on the school bus jeered at her when she got on, or how the girls in gym class avoided her. She was embarrassed. In college she became withdrawn and afraid of social situations, afraid that she would be ostracized in some way for being different, even though she grew to average height and developed a clearer complexion with the help of a dermatologist.

With use of the four "A" steps, she overcame embarrassment about her past and was able to tell her two close friends about her extreme fear of meeting new people and of entering a roomful of strangers. With help from her friends, she began to meet new people and finally established a relationship with a male classmate.

Some individuals have learning disabilities that they successfully hide because they feel ashamed. As adults, they never tell that they participated in special education classes during high school because of their dyslexia. There's Vanna, a dyslexic woman who couldn't learn to spell and avoided college because she had such a hard time reading. She avoided jobs that involved paperwork. She became a factory worker and was always careful not to let her co-workers know about her poor reading and spelling skills.

She hates being a factory worker. She knows that she is smarter than most of the people with whom she works. She wants a new job. She has become *aware* that she has been settling for less because she's ashamed of her secret. Now she's breaking free while taking the four "A" steps. She is now aware of how her situation came about and *accepts* responsibility for the situation. Her *alternatives* included staying stuck or look for a new job. Her fourth step, **Action,** currently involves going on job interviews.

Alcoholism vs. Self-Esteem

An arrest in 1992 for driving while intoxicated caused Roxanne Barton Conlin, an Iowa lawyer and president of the Association of Trial Lawyers of America, to make her alcoholism public. Her arrest emphasized to her that she was violating her own principles by getting behind the wheel of a car after drinking. "No one needed to tell me the risks. It's very hard to escape when you have done something that you have sued other people for, that you have told your children they must not do." She realized that she had a disease that could kill her and also others.

As a trial lawyer I led a very stressful life. I always had to be strong and powerful for others. But people who are trained to be tough think that to acknowledge a problem is to show weakness. The truth is that it takes strength to face our personal demons. Don't make the same mistake I did. Don't wait for an arrest or a tragedy to acknowledge that you need assistance.

I was a binge drinker and drank wine. My husband had suggested that I had a drinking problem, but for a long time I brushed off the idea. It was easy to hide. I was able to get drunk on just a few drinks. In fact, the night of my arrest I only had five glasses of wine. I recognized alcoholism as part genetic, part chemical, and totally involuntary, but I knew I had it. When my arrest hit the front page of the newspaper, I could no longer hide it. I acknowledged responsibility for my conduct; it was totally my fault. I apologized for the embarrassment to my family and friends and expressed relief that no one was hurt.

My recovery included attending AA meetings, reading books on the subject, and seeking counseling. It's easier to stay sober now because everybody knows my name, even flight attendants on airplanes. I'm proud of myself and know that now I have nothing to hide. I even wrote about my former addiction in my column in the Association of Trial Lawyers of America *monthly magazine.*

Abuse vs. Self-Esteem

Marsha is a high-powered executive but hides her alcoholism, drug use, and insecurity. She uses aggressiveness to overwhelm employees. She is tough. As a child she was picked on and was physically and verbally abused on the playground by other children because she had a deformed leg. In response to the abuse, she decided to become a bully herself.

Marsha is working on changing her aggressive behavior by using the material in earlier chapters of this book. She is working on her dependencies, too, and believes that when she feels more confident about herself she will be alcohol and drug-free.

Marsha is like many children who are picked on. They often show either of two basic types of responses: 1) become withdrawn, scared, introverted (flight) or 2) become a bully, aggressive, and tough (fight).

They want to keep everyone at a distance. They act very macho. As adults, it is important for such individuals to consider where some of their internal messages came from and rethink their life patterns. *Alternatives* are available. Choices can be made. New *actions* can be taken.

Time for Action

Keeping secrets may be holding you back from improving personal relationships, work situations, wellness, and other aspects of your life that are important to you. You've read about several people—perhaps very much like you—who have secrets. Some decided to tell and others chose to keep their secrets, but all consciously decided to stop letting their secret haunt them and burden and squash their power and self-esteem. After reading this chapter, perhaps you too will feel less squashed by the burden, less hurt, less haunted, and ready to move on with boosting your self-esteem.

9

TAKE CARE OF YOURSELF:
WELLNESS IS A BOOSTER

Feeling well is a booster. Taking good care of yourself is a booster. How well you take care of yourself is also a measure of how highly you value yourself.

Wellness has many definitions. It's taking care of your physical, emotional, and behavioral self. Here are a few definitions we've heard from women in group sessions:

> "It's more than absence of illness. It's a feeling of togetherness of mind, body and spirit."

> "Wellness is a successful management of lifestyle. It is being the best I can be."

> "It is peace and harmony with myself."

Feeling positive, good health, and self-esteem are all interrelated. You can't have any one without the others. When you feel good, you feel empowered. You have the energy you need to do what you want and enjoy what you do. When you have the energy and power to do what you want with gusto, your self-esteem rises.

Benefits of Good Health

Women with good health have more energy to get what they want out of life. Women who have strong self-esteem seem to worry less than others. One reason is that their mental outlook is healthier. They worry about worst-case scenarios less. Secondly, they are able to stand back and look at themselves. They are able to consider the Possible *Positive* Outcomes of taking risks, rather than listening to the self-defeating messages in their heads.

How often have you heard someone say "I was worried sick!" Worrying can make one sick! Worry is tension-filled, stress-producing mental work. Instead of worry, replace it with constructive thinking. Instead of thinking to yourself, "I have a problem!" think about what you can do to meet the problem head-on. Change your worry to positive action. Now that you know about the Womanpower four "A" Boosting Cycle of Awareness, Acceptance, Alternatives, and Action for boosting self-esteem, you can also put those same techniques to work for you in reducing worries in your life. You may start to feel healthier and more energetic!

Good health involves a healthy body, a sound mind, and a spiritual feeling that you are not only at one with yourself but also at peace within your universe.

HOW WELL DO YOU TAKE CARE OF YOURSELF?

Taking care of yourself is the best step toward good health. To take good care of yourself, you must like yourself. Liking yourself is an important factor in self-esteem. How will others like and respect you if you don't like yourself? LOVE yourself, and others will love you, too. Loving yourself means taking care of yourself—giving time and attention to things that keep you feeling good.

Realize that you are the most important person you know. There are certain things that only you can do for yourself. Only you control exactly what you eat or drink, whether or not you smoke, and how much exercise you do. Changing some of these habits may keep you healthy as well as boost your self-esteem!

The following quiz will help you determine how well you take care of yourself. Answer YES or NO to each question. (Some answers may not be so clear-cut, but do the best you can.) At the end of the test, you'll read about how to take better care of yourself, if you're not doing that already.

TAKING CARE OF YOURSELF

	YES	NO
Do you take time to eat nutritiously?		
Do you avoid compulsive overeating?		
Are you able to control your eating habits?		
Do you maintain a good weight for your size and body build?		
Do you like your body build and size?		
Do you exercise regularly?		
Do you get enough sleep?		
Do you sleep through the night?		
Do you go for a routine physical exam even if you are feeling fine?		

	YES	NO
Have you had a Pap test within the last year or two?		
Do you do breast self-examinations monthly?		
Do you visit your dentist when necessary?		
Do you follow recommendations of your dentist?		
Do you take prescribed medicine when advised?		
If you are over 40, have you had a baseline mammogram?		
If you are over 50, do you go for annual mammograms?		
Are you a non-smoker?		
Are you a non-drinker or a very moderate drinker?		
Do you occasionally let yourself relax in the bathtub?		
Do you have hobbies that give you pleasure?		
Do you treat yourself as well as you treat others?		
Are you a good friend to yourself?		
Do you do something nice for yourself regularly?		
Do you let other people do nice things for you?		

	YES	NO

Do you reward yourself
for personal
accomplishments?

If you answered YES to most of the above questions, it looks like you are taking good care of yourself. If you answered NO to more than 10 questions, look over the questions again and determine how you can start taking better care of yourself. When you take better care of yourself, you will feel better and feel a sense of increased personal wellness.

Boosted Self-Esteem Can Lead to Better Health

More women than men "internalize" their frustration and anger. Instead of showing it, they express it as passive aggression. That can lead to physical ailments. For some, this may be headaches, high blood pressure, stomachaches, or other symptoms. More women than men suffer from migraine headaches and irritable bowel syndrome, two conditions which seem to be largely influenced by repressed emotional feelings, especially anger.

Learn to listen to your own body. No one else can hear the signals just the way you do. Understand when your symptoms are caused by your own internal squashers, when self-defeating messages replayed in your head later turn into headaches and stomachaches. Your body sends you messages, such as continuing discomfort or pain. Some women try to resolve problems with "quick fixes," such as medication or alcohol. These routes can be hurtful, not helpful. Know when symptoms should be brought either to the attention of a medical or psychological clinician.

Keep Your Movable Parts Moving

Regular exercise can provide more than just benefits to your cardiovascular system and your muscles. It can also help clear your head. During exercise, certain body chemicals called endorphins are produced that can actually elevate your mood and energize you. Maybe you've heard the term "runner's high," or the "endorphin high." It is the body's natural healing drug. You don't have to be a marathon runner to get the same effect. Just taking a brisk walk for a mile or two, or swimming, can give you a high.

Other activities that give you a "natural high" include aerobic exercise, dancing, laughter, having fun. These activities help many women free themselves of anxieties and "the blues" caused by repeated, self-defeating messages. Relaxation therapy, guided imagery, and creative visualization are also healthy ways to learn to relax and take good care of your mind and your body.

In the last decades, regular exercise has become part of lifestyle for many. Less than a generation ago, one saw mostly men at the gym, but that's all changed. Taking care of our bodies has become not only necessary but fashionable! Walk into any health club now and you'll see women working on weights, sweating as they pedal stationary bicycles, or panting as they traverse an imaginary terrain on the treadmill. Aerobic exercise classes are provided for women of all ages, sizes and shapes, on land or in the water.

If you don't exercise, check out possibilities of aerobics classes. Many classes cater to overweight women, middle-aged and older women. Most classes have no special clothing requirements. Being a couch potato is out: healthy movement is in.

Eating for More Power

In many families, a mother puts her own food needs last, after considering possible special needs of her husband and her children. Remember your food needs are equally important. At different ages, women have needs for more iron, calcium, and other vitamins and minerals. A balanced diet, without excess calories, is essential at all ages.

Here's what some women say:

Rita

I was much thinner before my children were born. It wasn't that I was such a big eater, but I would finish all the food on the children's plates. I grew up during the Depression and believed that it was a sin to waste food. The sin was that I gained 40 pounds over a ten-year period. My children aren't fat, but I am.

When I was a child my parents used to say, "think of the starving people in China" if I left anything on my plate. That notion stuck in my head when I saw food left on my own kids' plates. Then I used food to swallow my anger about other aspects of my life, such as my relationship with my husband. I was bored and needed friendship but couldn't get out much to see other people. So food became my comfort, friend and source of pleasure. Now that I'm aware of how I got this way, I'm beginning to work on it.

Here's Cindy, the One Who "Swallowed Herself"

I couldn't trust myself. I was a compulsive overeater. I would buy a carton of ice cream, planning to serve it to guests the next day. As soon as I got home, I would devour the whole thing. That's why I tried not to keep much food at home, especially things like cakes or ice cream, I remember once

> *buying cookies in the supermarket. I ate them all while shopping. When I checked out, the bag was empty. I knew I had a problem. My overeating was caused by swallowing my feelings. Remember—I was called the Woman Who Swallowed Herself? To avoid my anxiety and confronting my issue, I would overeat.*

Eating three meals a day with a reasonable number of calories and low in fat is the best means of weight control for most people. On the other hand, women who try "crash" diets that omit many nutrients from the diet often find that their weight comes back. They don't learn meaningful life changes that are necessary to sustain weight loss.

A well-balanced breakfast helps you start your day on the right track. A slow release of necessary nutrients throughout the morning can keep your energy level up. However, if you eat a breakfast high in sugar content, you may have a sudden rise in blood sugar, but a rebound effect later in the morning will make you feel tired and send you looking for more sugary foods. Instead of waiting until you get to your office to have coffee and a sweet roll, take time at home (or go out) for some fruit or fruit juice, a bowl of cereal, and perhaps a grainy bread. You'll feel better all day long.

Space your meals throughout the day. Don't go longer than five hours without eating. If you don't have time for lunch, snack on lowfat foods, such as cut up vegetables, a piece of fruit, or a carton of lowfat yogurt. Drink lots of water. Keep some energizing snacks at the office or worksite. Avoid seeking out sweets and fatty snacks.

Don't be fooled by the caffeine in coffee. Caffeine may give you a temporary lift in the morning, but too much caffeine can cause symptoms resembling severe anxiety and panic attack. Many women get "caffeine" headaches, which come as a result of too much caffeine or too little. Some who have weekend headaches find that a cup of coffee relieves the headaches.

That's because during the week their caffeine consumption is higher early in the day. On weekends, they may not start their day until almost noon, and the body has missed its "caffeine fix."

How to Change Your Eating Habits

If you are like many women we know, changing habits isn't easy. But remember, it isn't an "all or nothing" situation. You don't have to change everything at once. Make one change at a time. Make a little change at a time. Here are some quick and easy tips that you may have heard before but which we think are basics that work for most of us:

- Select an appropriate place to eat at home or at work; eat only at that spot.
- Use a specific place setting. Set the table, even for snacks.
- Always sit down at your place setting. Don't eat standing up (e.g., at the refrigerator or kitchen sink). Don't eat while walking, while driving, or while watching TV.
- Eat slower. Wait until you have enough time to eat your planned meal or snack slowly.
- Plan your shopping list carefully. Don't shop while you are hungry. Avoid impulse buying.
- At parties, when you have a choice, select foods that are healthy rather than attractively prepared. For example, choose veggies with a yogurt dip instead of the tinted-pink cream cheese on little bread squares.
- Place yourself far from the buffet table to avoid nibbling food to cover any social anxieties you may be feeling. Talk to a person who is standing alone instead. (With self-esteem and assertiveness, you now feel confident and comfortable talking with new people, right?)

- At other people's homes, say NO to certain foods rather than trying to please the host or hostess. (Remember, YOU are the most important person you know.)

Think About Healthy Eating

This is a set of guidelines suggested by the American Dietetic Association (ADA) during the 1990s. This involves:

- 6–11 servings daily of foods from grains. These foods supply fiber, carbohydrates, vitamins, and minerals.
- 2–4 servings daily of fruit. This level includes foods from plants. Most people need to eat more fruits and vegetables for the vitamins, minerals, and fiber they supply.
- 3–5 servings of vegetables daily
- 2–3 servings daily of meat, poultry, fish, dry beans, eggs and nuts
- 2–3 servings of milk, yogurt, cheese. Foods in this category and the one above come mostly from animals. They are important sources of protein, calcium, iron, and zinc.
- Fats, oils, and sweets: use sparingly. This group includes salad dressings, oil, butter, margarine, cream, soft drinks, candy and sweet desserts. These foods provide calories and little else nutritionally.

Waist Management: Weight Control

Sheila:

I lost 45 pounds in a year. My secret: eat less and cut out the fat. I also exercised a lot. I jog and work out regularly at the health club.

What worked for Sheila can work for you, too. The first step is making a commitment. Losing some weight may be on your list of "wants." You may already have made a contract with yourself to start controlling your food, instead of having it control you. As a way of becoming aware of where your extra calories and fat grams are coming from, keep a food diary. Write down everything you eat. Put the item in one column, the time of day in the center, and how you were feeling at the time. (That's to check to see if it was lunchtime or late at night—when you were feeling down because the man you met last week hadn't called yet.)
Here's the form:

FOOD DIARY

ITEM   DAY, TIME   MOOD

Here's What Sheila Did to Lose Weight:

First, to eat less, I started by cutting every portion of food I considered eating in half and ate only that half, no matter what it was. If I felt like eating a whole gallon of frozen yogurt, I had half. Pretty soon I cut down on that, too. Then I realized I didn't need an expensive diet plan or to buy specially prepared foods. The diet centers can't do it all for you. You have to do it yourself. Go on a low-fat, low-cholesterol diet. I cut out as much fat as possible. It worked."

It's easier than you think. You can do it when you understand a few basics.
Fats are an important part of our diet. Fats have an important function. They conserve body heat, build new tissue, form hormones, promote growth of beneficial intestinal bacteria, and carry fat-soluble vitamins to all cells of the body. Most of us eat too much

dietary fat. Total fat intake should be less than 30 percent of our daily calories. If you reduce yours to that amount, and maintain it there, you will probably lose weight.

Soon it will be easier to determine quantities of fat in our diet when federal law requires a listing of grams of fat per serving and number of calories from fat on all food labels.

What about cholesterol? Your body makes enough cholesterol; you don't need to get it from what you eat. What do cholesterol levels mean?

Best cholesterol levels = 200 mg/dL or less

Your total cholesterol count is made up of Low-Density Lipoproteins (LDL) as well as High-Density Lipoproteins (HDL). The good ones are the LDLs; the baddies are the HDLs.

Typical healthy cholesterol profile:

Low-Density Lipoproteins (LDL) = 130 mg/dL or less

High-Density Lipoproteins (HDL) = 35 mg/dl or less

How to Cut Back on Fat and Cholesterol

Fats in foods make them tastier, juicier. That's why we like fat in our diet. Here's a list of suggestions you can use to cut the fat:

- Limit meat intake each day to 6 ounces or less (30 grams fat)
- Trim all visible fat before cooking
- Bake or broil meats; don't fry
- If you fry, use a vegetable spray instead of fat
- Remove skin from poultry, either before cooking or at the table
- Use skim milk and low-fat dairy products
- Use small amounts of oils and lowfat dressings

- Increase fiber by eating more fruits and vegetables
- Try to keep your fat intake to 30 percent of your total calories for each day

Eating Disorders

Serious eating disorders that can be life threatening include obesity, anorexia nervosa and bulimia. More women have these eating disorders than men. If you are one of them, get medical help. Get psychological counseling. It can save your life!

Unrealistic Body Image Created by Media

Public media squashes self-esteem for many women. Unfortunately, the American "ideal" of a woman's shape is unattainable. The ideal has been created by advertisers who use the bodies of teenagers to model clothes worn by women of all ages. Models' bodies are often augmented, pared, repaired, and even replaced. Did you know that in some movies, stars use whole-body stand-ins for close shots involving nudity? So the actress with the ideal face may not also have the perfect body, though we are led to believe otherwise. Too many women, particularly young women, starve themselves and exercise excessively to achieve what they perceive as the "perfect" body.

The current American ideal of slim, trim, fit bodies causes many women to compare themselves to models. Thinking they fall short of being attractive, many women lose their good image of themselves. Attitudes regarding female body proportions have increasingly led women to cosmetic surgery. The recent uptrend in breast augmentation as well as liposuction attests to interest in changing body shape, whether because of outside influences or women's critical self-perceptions.

Body Image and Life-Threatening Eating Disorders

Anorexia develops out of a fear of and perception that one is fat. It involves, literally, starving oneself in an effort to be thin. It can lead to hormonal changes that can cause delay of onset of menses or temporary cessation of menstruation. All this hormonal fluctuation isn't healthy. Bulimia (the binge and purge syndrome) can lead to serious loss of vitamins and minerals. And the burden of hiding this secret leads to additional stress and anxiety.

Many women have been helped with professional counseling. You can be, too.

Here's Julie's story:

> *I slowed down my eating in seventh grade. I wanted to be thin. I began to lose weight but nobody noticed. My parents would be busy talking at mealtime. When they did notice how little I ate, I would make some excuse. I did a lot of sit-ups and other exercises quietly in my room in an effort to lose even more calories. No one knew. When I was 14, my periods hadn't come and I was noticeably thin. My mother insisted I see our family doctor. Right away she suspected that I might be starving myself to stay thin. Afterward, I began therapy and slowly began to gain a little weight. I'm glad I did. That first visit to my doctor probably saved my life. I joined a support group. I've heard of many girls who died as a result of anorexic behaviors.*

Alcoholism and Drug Addictions

Women who are addicts may be so because they have turned to these substances as "quick fixes" either to cover their lack of self-esteem, to avoid anxiety, or to give themselves false boosters. An addict is not in control of her own body, her own health, or her own mind. She is the opposite of one who has Woman-power. Help is available. With appropriate commitment and help, she can turn her life around.

Here's Marnie, who overcame alcoholism:

My boost came when I accepted the fact that I used drinking to cover up my insecurities. I grew up in an alcoholic household. I saw my parents covering up for everything that was wrong by hitting the old bottle. I wanted out of that pattern. The first step was mine, by being aware of my addiction, accepting responsibility for it, looking at alternatives of lifestyle and taking action. The action I took was joining and sticking with AA.

What Is Stress?

Everyone has stress. Stress is your body's reaction to external stimuli (called stressors) that cause physiological changes in your body's natural rhythms. Those external stresses in our lives are like dominoes. One thing leads to another, and another, and pretty soon we feel totally knocked down. You may feel unable to cope with everyday problems, find it difficult to get along with people, trapped and inadequate. When you don't feel support from those around you as you try to tackle the issues you face, your stress may increase.

We all need strong, effective, inner coping mechanisms. Those who have them, deal well with stress. Without good coping mechanisms, many people feel overwhelmed by small things.

Stress is a part of everyday life. We all feel a sense of emotional strain, anxiety, and tension at times. We each experience life in unique ways, so what is a source of stress for one person may not be for another. What causes one person to go to "overload" may not affect another person at all.

What causes stress? Reasons differ between individuals. Some find happy events, such as planning a trip, starting a new job, moving to a new house, getting married—big sources of stress. Others find that difficulties between individuals in their home life or at work causes stress. Of course, major life changes, such as the death of a loved one or divorce cause stress for most people.

There are self-induced stressors, such as feeling a need to be "Superwoman" at work and at home. The women who want to "have it all" and have unreasonable expectations of themselves feel stressed. Those who learn to delegate responsibilities and don't expect perfection of themselves or others cope the best.

What Happens During a Stressful Situation?

Your whole body chemistry changes during stress. Your nervous system goes into high gear. Your adrenaline starts flowing. Your "fight or flight" response becomes activated, and several of your internal systems get going. For example, certain hormones, such as adrenaline and insulin, increase their flow. This leads to a quickened heartbeat, rapid breathing, and sweating.

The stress response is often brought on over a period of time. After a while, it takes longer for the body to return to its routine chemical state of balance. Continued imbalance can lead to illness. As a result, the negative consequences of long-term stress can be illnesses such as ulcers and other digestive disorders, high blood pressure (hypertension), musculoskeletal problems, diabetes, and psychological disorders such as depression and extreme anxiety.

At one time in our history, this response was helpful to escape from dangers such as wild animals, but now the physical need to fight or flee is usually not necessary (except in cases of real-life danger, etc.). This same reaction causes energy to become trapped inside our bodies, and this can lead to emotional or physical illness. Some people overreact. For example, they have bigger reactions to "perceived" danger and stay in the stress response too long, which may lead to a physical problem.

Stress affects people in different ways. Here's what one woman says: "When I feel really stressed, I get a sick feeling in the pit of my stomach. Sometimes my hands and feet go numb. It feels like my heart is pounding."

Some people thrive on stress. Some say that stress raises their energy level and helps them focus their mind better. In fact, some people are often attracted to high-stress occupations and professions. When reacted to in a healthy way, stress can motivate and make you more productive. Stress from work can spill over into your home life, and stress from home can affect your work.

Tips on Coping with Stress

- Change worry and guilt to direct action. Either do something directly to change the problem or reassess the problem and discover that you can perceive the situation differently.

- Realize that several people are attempting to cope with their own stress and the stress of others they care about.

- The closer the relationship, the more important the other's stress is for you.

- Learn to separate various stressors and deal with one at a time.

- Learn relaxation techniques.

- Prioritize your projects. Set realistic goals for yourself. Understand your own coping skills with stressors.

- Don't catch the ball marked guilt when it is thrown to you. Remember, catching the ball is your choice.

- Change unreal expectations to realistic expectations.
- Learn to say NO. You can't be all things to all people.

Don't use the word "breakdown." Machines break down. We experience emotions and feelings. Learn to use anger effectively: For example, instead of getting angry while waiting in a long supermarket checkout line, pick up a magazine and get engrossed in it for a few minutes. The line will seem to move faster. People who are resentful all the time damage themselves.

Extremely Unusual Events That Cause Stress

If you have been exposed to sudden and unexpected events, such as witnessing a crime or being a victim yourself, or surviving a natural disaster such as a flood, fire, or earthquake, you may have symptoms for weeks or months or longer. You may not have symptoms until years later. Your mind and body may continue to react in many ways. You may have bad dreams, flashbacks, and feelings that the event is recurring. You may have difficulty concentrating. During this period, you may be extremely vulnerable to many anxieties and fears. You may even avoid activities you once enjoyed. Often a person copes for a long time and then develops symptoms later. For example, women who have been molested, experienced incest or rape, including date rape, may actually suffer from what is known as post-traumatic stress disorder (PTSD) later on. To get through such a period of life, professional help may be necessary.

There are no quick fixes, but small improvements may help you feel better. Until you obtain help (or as an addition to any type of therapy you do receive), you may apply the four "A" steps of Womanpower to your situation: Become Aware of your responses. Accept the fact that you have behaviors you would like to change. Consider Alternative behaviors, and then take Action.

Low Self-Esteem Leads to Depression

We all feel a little down occasionally. We get the "blues." Some women who have premenstrual syndrome experience a very low, sad mood before their periods. But clinical depression is a more serious matter. Unfortunately, depression affects about one of every nine of us at some times in our lives. There is situational depression, in which we experience a feeling of deep depression in response to a specific event, such as after the death of a loved one or being fired from a job. Such a depression has an identifiable beginning and usually comes to an end on its own, such as after the mourning period or finding another job. Depression of this type is known as "exogenous" depression, which means that it comes from outside sources.

There is a type of clinical depression known as "endogenous" depression that comes from within. For many people, this is caused by a chemical imbalance in the brain. This can be overcome with a combination of psychotherapy and carefully supervised medication. It cannot be overcome with self-medication or alcohol. Such quick fixes only make it worse and lead to complications.

How can you tell the difference between "the blues" and serious depression? Feeling down happens to all of us for various reasons. Teenagers who don't get invited to parties, women whose jobs are terminated, women in the process of a divorce, or after a death in the family, experience feeling down, or worse, "being in a black hole."

Depression includes ongoing feelings of self-worthlessness, lack of self-importance, extreme hopelessness, and helplessness. Depressed people see no way out. They see no alternatives. There may be thoughts of suicide. This may go on for weeks, months, or longer.

If you know a woman suffering from serious, clinical depression, advise her to get help. If it's you, give yourself the power to take control. Take care of yourself.

Here's Rona's experience with depression:

> *I felt like I was always swimming upstream and never getting anywhere. I would look around me and see others doing things easily, which I found impossible. I just couldn't get going. I felt like I was fighting my way through a fog. Sometimes it just looked like darkness everywhere. Nothing looked clear to me. It took me a long time to do anything, even getting myself going in the morning. I felt like I had a weight on me. I finally realized that if I could just shed this weight—and I don't mean pounds—I could get out of my hole. I did, with help from a therapist.*

For many other women, low self-esteem is a common factor in depression. If you feel "down," helpless, hopeless, and stuck, learn to understand the differences between situational depression, which may last for a short period of time (after a major event, e.g., death of a spouse, divorce, etc.), or a more pervasive depression that can't be traced to an event, and which lasts for months or longer. Know the difference between "the blues" and a more serious situation. Learn the signs that indicate when ordinary boosters won't help and professional help many be necessary.

Here's Marion, the Non-Self:

> *I was a college student, severely depressed, stressed, and had arthritis in my fingers and neck. This was particularly unpleasant because my favorite hobby was playing the organ and piano. I*

*was working toward a degree in music therapy. I
came to understand that the arthritis was made
worse because I held back my extreme anger
toward my husband, who was having an affair. I
was afraid to leave him or even to get mad at him
outwardly, so I held my anger inside. That led to
both depression and physical illness. My self-
esteem was as squashed as one could imagine.
My therapist called me "the person with the non-
self."*

Marion learned to boost her feelings of power and
self-esteem to the point where she realized she had the
right to get angry at her husband and did not have to
put up with his very unpleasant and abusive behavior.
She knew she deserved better. After years of therapy
and assertiveness training, she finally divorced her
husband and finished her degree in music therapy—
and now her arthritis pain bothers her much less. She
has a new husband who treats her well.

Dealing Effectively with Anger

A few words about anger. Many angry people in the
world were battered, hurt, or ignored when they were
young. They felt victimized, helpless, or powerless to
do anything about it. They developed deep resentment at an early age.

If you believe that you live with some deeply rooted
anger, ask yourself if your current anger is "old stuff"
and out of proportion to your situation today, or if it
is anger over a current situation? If it is "old stuff,"
then that anger is a squasher for your self-esteem
because it reduces your effectiveness. Understand
your own anger, where it comes from, and what it is
about.

One way to deal with anger is to reduce expectations of others, as well as yourself. Realize that people
have individual differences. Other people may not do
things exactly the way you do. Be more tolerant. Be

more accepting. Also understand that you may get the angriest at the people you care about the most. That's because you have an emotional investment in your relationship with them. When your expectations are threatened, you feel the worst.

When You Need Professional Help

Sometimes stress, anxiety, fear, or anger become overwhelming. If you ever feel that you just cannot cope with what you face, and you have worked through the four "A" steps and think you need something stronger, look toward professional counseling. Taking a step toward obtaining professional counseling is taking care of yourself. It is a step you can take with strength after you have worked through the four "A" steps.

Good mental health is a continuum. Everyone has good days and bad, stresses brought on by work and home life, and moods that seem "down" from one's usual feeling of well-being. There are many women with serious mental-health concerns that get in the way of their self-esteem. You may be one of them, or you may know someone like this. If as a result of reading this book and thinking about the four "A" steps, you realize that more than self-help is necessary for the serious self-esteem issues (depression, post-traumatic stress disorder, abuse, incest, etc.), you may ask yourself, Where do I go and what type of therapist should I seek?

There are many levels of skilled therapists. You might want to talk with friends who have benefited from counseling—and ask them about their therapists. Some will tell you about psychiatrists, psychologists, social workers, marriage and family therapists, or addictions professionals. If you don't want to talk with friends, ask a health practitioner, such as your family physician, for a referral. Ask about the counselor's background, credentials, training, and affiliations with schools or hospitals.

Also, there are professional societies for many specialties. Check with an appropriate organization to see that the therapist has the appropriate accreditation to counsel in your community. Watch newspapers for announcements of seminars by therapists. Attend a workshop given by a local therapist. Get a sample of the therapist's style. Join a support group and meet others with similar concerns; some support groups are organized by competent therapists. Seek a therapist who seems empathetic—one who makes you feel comfortable talking about your self-esteem concerns.

Here's a brief run-down on non-medical types of mental-health professionals according to Ada P. Kahn and Jan Fawcett, M.D., authors of *The Encyclopedia of Mental Health* (Facts on File, N.Y., 1993):

Psychologists: Clinical psychologists have Ph.D.s in psychology. Some specialize in certain areas, such as marital therapy, eating disorders, child psychology, phobias, or drug addiction. Some therapists with Master's degrees also are known as psychologists. Clinical psychologists are usually licensed by the state in which they practice.

Social workers: Usually social workers have a Master's degree in social work as well as extensive training in a clinical setting. Some work in clinics or hospitals, and others work in private practice. They help people with a wide variety of concerns.

Family therapists: Marital and family therapists may be psychologists or social workers who specialize in helping couples or families cope with or prevent problems.

Addictions professionals: Depending on their training and state regulations, addictions professionals may be known as certified alcohol and drug counselors. These professionals may work in substance-abuse programs, weight-control programs, clinics, or hospitals. Often they work in conjunction with medical practices.

Seek counseling wisely. There are many mental-health professionals available to help you. Shop for a counselor just as you shop for a physician or dentist. If you need help, take that step: choose one and begin counseling. You may need to try more than one to find the right "fit." Choose wisely. You deserve the best. In many cases, short-term therapy may be all that is necessary to get you back on a sound emotional track. Remember, getting professional help for a mental-health concern is all part of taking good care of yourself.

Feeling Power, Feeling Good

Marion

> It's like I'm easily floating on the water, not fighting to keep my head above. When I walk, there's a string that holds my head up. I stand up straight now. I'm like a flower, or a butterfly, reaching up to the sunshine. When my new husband holds me, I'm so totally at peace with myself and my world. Is that love? Is that self-esteem? I can't believe it's Me. I finally like Me."

Rona

> When I got my new job, I felt so good. My headaches stopped. I realized that I was worth something to a business. I started appreciating Me.

Women who have boosted self-esteem are proud of themselves. They want to look as good as possible. They take care of themselves. They feel and look confident, stand tall, and look you in the eye when they speak. Women who feel good about themselves look more attractive to others. We communicate self-esteem through body language—standing erect or sitting up straight in school, business, or social situations—and this helps us project our level of self-esteem. People who are fearful show it. But confidence shows, too, in a much more powerful and favorable way.

Here's what Ada says about standing tall:

> *Having been 5'11" nearly all of my life, I finally realized that a tall woman can't hide her height. It's there. When a tall woman tries to conceal her height by slouching, people think, "There's a tall woman with bad posture." If she stands tall, they think, "There's an attractive tall woman who stands nice and straight." I keep my good posture. It's important to me. Also, since I've become more comfortable with my height, I've also come to a conclusion that since I'll be noticed, why not give people more to notice, such as big earrings, or brightly colored clothes. That's the new me.*

An Empowered Woman Loves Herself from Head to Toe

No matter what age you are, you are the most important person you know. You are special. There is no one else exactly like you. Love yourself. Be kind to yourself. Be your own heroine. Take time for yourself. Empower yourself. Give some nurturing to yourself, just as you do for others. No matter what your responsibilities to others are, do loving things for yourself. This may mean taking some time each day to read, to take a soothing bath or to go for a relaxing walk. You deserve it.

When you take care of yourself and feel good, you can deal confidently with all the changes life has in store for you. You will feel "centered," that you are in

control of yourself and your universe. You should be.
You deserve to be.

Give Yourself a Rose

Our friend, Kristin Lems, of Evanston, Illinois, is a
singer-songwriter. She composed the song, "She Gave
Herself a Rose," which she recorded on a compact
disc—UPBEAT!—produced by Carolsdatter Produc-
tions, Inc. in Evanston, Illinois. Her song was in-
spired by Rebecca Armstrong, another Chicago-based
folk singer. The lyrics to this song exemplify what we
mean by taking care of yourself, being kind to yourself, and loving yourself. (Emphasis added by us, not
the songwriter.)

She Gave Herself a Rose*
by Kristin Lems

When Rebecca came over to visit one day
She cheered up her friends in a most special way.
In honor of beauty and friendship and health,
She brought each a rose, and saved one for herself.

Chorus:
She gave herself a rose, she gave herself a rose
Strong but delicate, a treat for the nose.
She gave herself a rose, she gave herself a rose
Elegant gift of love, she gave herself a rose.

She said, "I once waited for some prince to come
Bearing roses and kisses, indeed I've had some,
But love has its seasons, it comes and it goes
But beauty must never die, long live the rose."

Chorus:
She gave herself a rose, she gave herself a rose
Strong but delicate, a treat for the nose.
She gave herself a rose, she gave herself a rose
Elegant gift of love, she gave herself a rose.

If your wings have been dragging, your smile has
   come loose
Treat yourself sweetly, you need no excuse.
You can be your best friend, and God only knows
You deserve all the best, so just give yourself a rose.

Chorus:
Give **yourself** a rose, give **yourself** a rose
Strong but delicate, a treat for your nose
Give **yourself** a rose, give **yourself** a rose
Elegant gift of love, just give **yourself** a rose.

10

GROWING OLDER, GROWING WISER!

Start preparing now to be a healthy, content, and happy woman. Whatever your age, take care of yourself. Give yourself boosters. Striving for self-esteem will never be easier than it is now. This is a chapter for you and for you to share with others. Sharing ideas about self-esteem helps build bridges for effective communication between generations of women. Self-esteem is something we all care about.

It's a Small World

Ada

A few years ago I was in Paris. During a walk, I happened upon a movie company filming a scene across the street from a small park. I sat down on a bench to watch the action. Soon I became aware of a woman sitting at the other end of the bench, also engrossed in watching the actors. She turned to me. With a twinkling laugh, she said, "Quel histoire" (What a story). Her name was Madelaine. We agreed that the chase scene, like movies, was indeed an illusion. We exchanged conversation about our lives, families, and work, and our reasons for being there at that moment in

226

the park, watching the filming. She was a museum curator, with a specialty in maps, and worked in a nearby Paris museum. She had been in her job for fifteen years, since her divorce. Now she lived alone but often saw her two grown children. She always walked two miles after lunch for exercise and usually enjoyed this particular spot for a quiet rest. She said the spot usually made her feel at peace, but not today, because of the moviemakers.

We shared a few moments of silence as the action across the street resumed. I watched her and the filming at the same time. She looked like a healthy person who spent a good amount of time outdoors. She was trim, her face was very smooth with a hint of a suntan; she had short, wavy, gray hair, and wore a stylish business suit and mid-heeled shoes. I guessed she was in her mid-50's. Just as I was starting to think about how alike our lives were, she turned to me again.

"What do Americans think about gray hair?" she asked.

I told her that it seemed to me that most of us don't like it. In fact, a majority of women over age 50 who have gray hair probably hide the gray by coloring their hair. We think gray hair is a sign of age. We don't like to look old. We want to look younger than we are. Especially women. Women, particularly single women, don't think men will look at them if they have gray hair. It's okay for men to have gray hair, because women think men with gray hair look distinguished.

"Quel dommage" (What a shame), she said, with a grand, flourishing arm gesture. "In France, it is not a problem. French women do not mind having gray hair. French men think older women are attractive. They do not notice gray hair. It is what is in here (covering her heart with both hands) that counts."

Since that time, I have thought about Madelaine and how she projected strong self-esteem. What made me think so? What were the signals? She seemed to take good care of herself and got some exercise every day by walking to offset the sitting she did at her museum job. She was proud of how she looked. She believed that her work was important, and she enjoyed her work. She had a good relationship with her children. She spoke affectionately of her elderly mother who also lived in Paris. She viewed her past marriage as one of many stages of life through which she had moved. She valued her opinions as well as those of others. She felt free to express herself. She didn't put anyone else down. She always looked forward, not backward. She was open to new ideas.

Could it be that French women's feelings of inner peace enables them to grow older with grace—and gray hair? Does their high sense of self-esteem enable them to project a confident image? Are they more accepting of their changing appearance as they grow older than American women? Female anatomy is the same; changes happen at midlife. The physical changes are the same, so the differences must be in perception.

Perhaps one difference is that French women look at themselves and the world around them in a different way than Americans do. For example, the French women who enjoyed an active life in their youth continue to see themselves as vibrant, attractive, and feminine. On the other hand, some older American women view themselves as "old, overweight, and not attractive."

Madelaine appreciates herself for what and who she is. I believe that her gesture of crossing her hands over her chest was a sign that said,

*"here is the center of my strength." Her feeling of
self-appreciation helps her achieve a feeling of
balance within herself and with her universe. She
understands the connection between her mind,
through self-esteem and good health, by taking
care of her body. And she projects a sense of
"wholeness" by being open, outgoing, accepting,
and confident. She likes people and people are
attracted to her.*

Self-Esteem: A Concern at All Ages

Do you think that self-esteem is an issue just for
young people? No way! Young women reading this
may be surprised to learn that older people may have
even more self-esteem concerns. This was evidenced
in a 1992 Gallup poll for *Newsweek* magazine in
which more older people indicated feeling badly
about themselves than younger ones when asked the
same questions. For example, in response to the
question, "Which situations would make you feel
very bad about yourself," here's the breakdown by
age groups for a few key questions:

SELF-ESTEEM AT ALL AGES

	AGE 18–29	30–49	50 AND OVER
Being criticized by someone you admire	19%	19%	39%
Doing something embarrassing in public	26%	25%	50%
Being noticeably overweight	39%	29%	42%

	AGE		
	18–29	30–49	50 AND OVER
Not being able to pay your bills	51%	57%	80%

Self-esteem is a lifetime quest. There are particular challenges to Womanpower and self-esteem at all ages. It all begins in girlhood. For many, such as the respondents to the 1991 American Association of University Women survey, self-esteem is squashed by the end of adolescence. According to *Shortchanging Girls, Shortchanging America* (AAUW, 1991): "As girls and boys grow older, both experience a significant loss of self-esteem in a variety of areas; however, the loss is most dramatic and has the most long-lasting effect for girls. Adolescence, the period of transition from childhood to adulthood, is a critical time for the development of self-identity. It is one of the stages of a person's life where changes in biology and psychology are dramatic. It is a critical moment of a person's life to make a broad set of choices and decisions. And, finally, it is the time in a person's life when the differences of gender are particularly formative for the adult lives of women and men in our society."

Growing Up with Womanpower

Do you have a preteen or teenage daughter or granddaughter with whom you can share what you are learning about self-empowerment? Young women in this age group face particular challenges. They may still have many childhood interests and attitudes, and at the same time want to behave as an adult and be accepted as such.

Adolescence is a time of physiological and psychological changes. For example, some young women may develop secondary sexual characteristics earlier or later than others. Some girls who still have "pancake" chests at age 11 may feel less confident than friends who wear and fill out bras. Girls who have acne feel less confident than their clear-faced companions. Listen to Jennifer, the daughter of one of our 40-year-old friends:

> *I'm 14 and going to a dermatologist for my acne. At first I thought no one would want me at parties. But boys have zits, too. They understand. Now I tell myself, I'm Jennifer, I do have acne . . . and I'm an intelligent, likable, lovable person who is fun to have at parties. I still like me, but I'll like the way I look more when I have clearer skin.*

If you have a young person with whom to share your new excitement about gaining Womanpower, try the following self-test to determine where she stands on the Growing Up, Growing Wiser scale. Ask her to answer the following questions with a YES or NO wherever possible. (Some answers may not be as definite as YES or NO, but ask her to do the best she can.) YES answers mean that she is moving up on the Womanpower scale. NO answers mean that she should start planning now to empower herself. Many of the same self-help techniques you have been reading about in this book may help her.

At the end of the test, she will be able to recognize areas in her life in which she can give her feelings of empowerment a boost by using the four "A" steps:

- Awareness
- Acceptance
- Alternatives
- Action

QUIZ FOR YOUNG WOMEN

GROWING UP, GROWING WISER SCALE

	YES	NO

Do you feel as smart as others in your class?

Do you feel as capable as others?

Do you have career goals?

Do you believe that you can reach the goals you set?

Do you make a good effort to overcome obstacles in your way?

In social situations, do you find it easy to meet people?

Are you able to enjoy good conversations on many topics with people your age as well as older adults?

Do you like the way you look?

Do you think you look as good as others your age?

Is your current weight ok?

Do you dress appropriately for various situations?

	YES	NO
Do you enjoy being with young men?		
Do you know how to protect yourself from unwanted pregnancy and sexually transmitted diseases?		
Do you feel supported in emotional ways by family and friends?		
Do you talk openly with family and friends about your current school activities?		

If you answered YES to most of the above questions, you are well along on the "growing up, growing wiser" scale. You feel good about yourself, you are on a good track, you have ambition and ideals, and you are empowered to get ahead. If you answered NO to more than 8 of the questions, take a minute to think about how you can turn the NO answers into YES by changing your attitudes, behaviors, or situations in positive ways.

The Juggling Act: Working Mothers

Are you a working mother? (If you are not, perhaps you have a friend with whom you can share the quiz that follows on page 237.) Some women who work put their own self-esteem at risk by expecting too much from themselves. For example, some expect perfection in all aspects of keeping their family, home, and work life in order. Some have self-doubts and feel less than equal to all their tasks. Some try to be "Super

Mom" and just can't live up to their own expectations. An example of a squasher such women give themselves is, "I try to do all these things, but I just can't keep up. I'm just not a good mother." The booster is: "I'm Mary, and I work hard at keeping the house nice, my family satisfied, my job done well . . . and so what if everything isn't done perfectly, I'm doing the best I can, my family loves me, my boss thinks everything is alright."

Midlife Women CAN Be Better Than Ever

Are you a midlife woman? (If you are not, maybe you have a Midlife Mom with whom you can share this chapter.) Many women at midlife feel that they are ready for a new beginning. Once their childbearing and possibly child-raising years are over, they finally have time to do what they want. If you are in this age group, make the most of your years ahead. You may have a third of your life ahead of you.

On the other hand, some midlife women question their self-worth at this time. Some feel less needed when their children leave home. Some feel less attractive and know that their husbands see attractive, younger women everyday in the workplace. Some women who are alone because of divorce or widowhood feel like "fifth wheels" at social occasions. ("They don't want me here; they don't need me here.")

Body shape changes at midlife. Women need a good sense of humor. We have a friend who looked in the mirror one day and said to herself, "I never was so short-waisted. My waist is shorter." Then she looked again and decided that "My waist isn't shorter; my boobs are longer!"

Body image becomes even more important at middle age. Some women feel less attractive when their waists get a little wider after menopause. Hair color becomes important; many feel less attractive when their hair turns gray. We like the attitude of the gray-haired Parisian Madelaine, who feels attractive and projects confidence.

Sheila and the Big 50

While working on this book, Sheila hit the big 50 (Ada already passed it), making her reflect on growing older and wiser:

> *I'm older and wiser now. I've always felt young and always exercised a lot. Now I'm compulsive about exercise because it's the way to keep my body looking youthful and me feeling good. I recognize that my values and goals have changed. I used to push myself and often worked sixty hours a week, including teaching at every college around. I realize now that I was out to prove that I was okay. I was overcompensating. Now I'm more selective about what I do. I want more time with my friends. Now it's important to me to build relationships with friends. I want to change my career, do less psychotherapy and more public speaking.*

Midlife Myra and Her Money

Are any of you like Myra, who doesn't know about managing money? She says she is "financially un-aware" and is now determined to make changes in her life.

> *I feel personally "unfinished." Money is an area of my life that I know little about. My husband always took charge of our finances. A few years ago I secretly opened my own account at a local bank so I would have "my own money." I hid the account from my husband. When I went to make a withdrawal, I found that the monthly service charges had taken a big bite from the account. I felt like the little helpless girl I was in college*

when my father always wired money into my account. This time I had to call my husband and ask him what to do. I felt like I had become my mother, who never knew anything about managing money.

I'll Be 54 Anyway!

Our friend Emily Sloane, of Evanston, Illinois, is an example of an empowered, mature woman who met a challenge with success and satisfaction. Now she's retired from an eighteen-year career using her law background.

The youngest of Emily's three sons started junior high school when Emily was 50. For the first time in years, no one would come home for lunch and Emily's days would be completely free. She decided that a law degree could be used in many ways and applied to law school. "People were disbelieving. They were quite astonished. Back in 1970, this just wasn't being done by women of my age. One friend said, 'You'll be fifty-four years old when you graduate.' So what, I said. I'll be fifty-four anyway!"

Studying law was a big challenge and it was hard. We put in long hours, and it was physically and mentally challenging. To do something hard when you're fifty is good.

I had a good example of a woman who was vigorous at an older age: my mother. (Read about Emily's mother, Floy, on page 240.) My mother gave me lifelong boosters. From early grade school and on she told me I was smart and could do whatever I set out to do.

⫸⫷⫸⫷⫸⫷⫸⫷⫸⫷⫸⫷⫸⫷⫸⫷⫸⫷⫸⫷

SELF-TEST: FOR WOMEN OVER AGE 45

Please answer the following questions with YES or NO answers.

GROWING OLDER, GROWING WISER—AFTER AGE 45

	YES	NO
Do you think you are as capable as you were when you were younger?		
Do you think of yourself as attractive?		
Do you think you look as good as other women your age?		
Are you pleased with your job situation?		
Do you exercise regularly?		
Are you doing your best to avoid osteoporosis?		
Do you have ambitions you want to fulfill in the next few years?		
Do you have plans for your life as you move toward retirement age?		

⫸⫷⫸⫷⫸⫷⫸⫷⫸⫷⫸⫷⫸⫷⫸⫷⫸⫷⫸⫷

If you answered YES to most of the above questions, you are well along toward growing older wisely. If you answered NO to any questions, try to analyze how you can make those NO situations more positive by changing your habits or attitudes. Growing older wisely is growing older as an empowered woman with self-esteem.

Midlife Caregivers

Statistics show that today's women will spend more time in caring for aging parents than they did in raising their own children. How one deals with this aspect of life can influence one's self-esteem. For example, in the support group for caregivers of aging parents in our women's health program, we have many women who are well over 65 years old themselves. They have the responsibility for a parent or parents, and often for two households. Many feel overburdened, have no time for themselves, and feel guilty when they want time to take care of themselves.

Improvements in health care have created a situation in which more adult children are caring for parents at home for many years. Along with this responsibility comes a tremendous amount of emotional pressure. Caregivers feel torn between their own life and the needs of their aging parents. Some say the situation makes them angry, depressed, or guilty. Some say they long for freedom from these responsibilities but feel guilty for wanting their freedom. At any age, anger, depression, and guilt can squash your self-esteem. For many women, the stress caused by these feelings isn't healthy. However, many midlife women have come to grips with the realities of their situations and make the most of it. Maxine has done just this:

> *I've been watching out for my mother now for about eight years. She's 89 and still manages to live alone. Since my daughters have been old enough to drive, they help me do her shopping and prepare her medications. One of us goes every day. We call it doing our Bubbe Duty. It*

makes us feel good to share the responsibilities.
By pulling together this way, my Mom can stay
independent and feel good about herself.

Retirement

Are you a retiree? Are you one of the lucky ones
who now have time to pursue what you always wanted
to do? We hope so. It should be a wonderful time of
life, if you have the health to enjoy it.

Unfortunately, some women who retire from the
workforce express feelings of reduced self-esteem
because they no longer feel needed. Some working
women say, "My career is my identity. I get my self-
esteem from my work." Many women who got their
boosters from their work say they miss having the
frequent good strokes from co-workers. They feel they
are no longer contributors to society.

There are still many boosters out there! You can
contribute valuable services as a volunteer and derive
satisfaction from hobbies. If you are in midlife and
not ready to retire, plan now! Martha has empowered
herself:

I'm 78 years old. I'm a widow, and my children
and their children are grown up. I stay in touch
with all of them in one way or another, even if it's
just to share recipes. It gives my grandchildren a
sense of family history to be able to prepare the
same dishes I've been serving for so many years.
When they ask for something, I feel important.

Taking good care of yourself and your appearance is
important as you grow older. You may say to yourself,
I don't go out much anymore. Why should I do this or
that? Why? Here's Esther:

A wise older friend once told me "you can wear a
very inexpensive dress and look lovely if your hair

looks right." I'm 82 and I still go to the beauty shop every week to have my hair done. It gives me a boost.

Successful Aging

Ada:

In 1981, I was assigned to interview a successful old ager for Your Health & Fitness *magazine. I chose my good friend Floy, who was then 90, because I thought she was a "model" senior adult. Now I realize that she was a successful old ager because she had Womanpower. She had self-esteem, which had developed throughout her lifetime. However, as a young woman, her career interests had been squelched by her mother. This was back around 1910 when her mother told her that she was too "weak and frail" to become a nurse. She never became a nurse, but raised children, grandchildren, and a great-grandchild, ran a bookstore, and taught Sunday school. In her 80s, she encouraged her own 50-year-old daughter to become a lawyer. Here are some excerpts from that feature:*

Q. People who know you say you are always cheerful and full of good humor. How do you manage to be that way?

A. When things strike me funny, I laugh. There's usually a good laugh in most situations. People get more out of life with a sense of humor. There's more to laugh at than to cry over. You know, laughter can be good medicine. I agree with Norman Cousins who wrote the book about laughing himself well.

Q. You started a new career at age 70. How did that happen?

A. About seven years after my husband died, I needed something to occupy my time and to provide some income. My experience of taking care of children seemed useful to young parents. So I started baby-sitting and developed a regular clientele of families. I'm still in touch with some of my babies. Some are over 21 years old now. But I never told anyone then that I was 70 at the time. If I told them, they would have worried about me getting on the bus to come to their homes. I think doing a lot of walking with young children and spending time in the park was good for me.

Q. Does faith in religion sustain you?

A. I haven't been a churchgoer in years, but I am a believer. I think people who don't believe in something larger than themselves are the unhappiest. You'd be surprised how many aren't believers.

Q. Do you think there's any secret about longevity?

A. If there is, it must be some amount of luck, and maybe more important, genes. I'm lucky to have survived four bouts with pneumonia. I still have all my senses. I hear well, enjoy smelling the flowers in the yard, and the taste of a good barbecued rib. I don't see so well, but after my surgery, that may change. Old age without all your senses can be pretty tragic. That's only being half alive.

Q. Is it difficult for an older person to adjust to living with a daughter's family?

A. I've lived with my daughter and her family now for seven years. It takes a lot of flexibility on all parts. We all have to make compromises. When I moved into the house, the three grandchildren had grown up and left. There were only two other adults around. We never make unreasonable demands on each other. I have adequate privacy. I go about as I please.

Q. Why do you think some older people show poor control of their dispositions?

A. That happens at any age. It seems that naturally bad dispositions increase with age. People should be more optimistic. Look on the bright side of things. Some always manage to feel sorry for themselves. However, if your health is good, it's easier to have a good disposition.

Q. What's your greatest disappointment?

A. I always wanted to write a cookbook. I loved to cook and saved recipes and thought when I retired I would write the book. Now I haven't been able to do it because of my vision. Perhaps I can do it after I have my cataract surgery.

Q. What gives you most satisfaction these days?

A. Being with young people. I guess I have never grown up. I enjoy my five grandchildren and two great-grandchildren, their husbands, wives, and friends, even though they are all over the country. The biggest thrill is seeing my great-grandchildren; the son of the grandson I raised is now 11. The other great-grandchild is two. My mother had twenty-two grandchildren. Recently my family had a reunion. There were 50 people. Keeping in touch with them is like an ongoing novel.

Floy died in March 1993. She was 101 years old. Her spirit lives on in the power she engendered in all whose lives she touched.

11

THE BIG BOOST:
BE YOUR OWN HEROINE

While reading this book, you have discovered a lot about your self-esteem, how it developed or didn't develop and how it was boosted or squashed. You have learned some tips on how to change your own squashers into boosters that work well for you. You have learned about the bounce-back messages and how to give yourself positive messages, looking toward Possible Positive Outcomes that may occur when you allow yourself to take risks and make changes.

You have learned to feel proud of yourself as a woman, to value yourself, and to go after what you want in life in personal as well as professional relationships. You have also developed a better understanding of how important good emotional and physical health are to your self-esteem.

We hope you have worked through the quizzes in various chapters and have discovered some truths about yourself to help you lead a more powerful and satisfying life. Use this book as a reinforcer. Return to it often. Boosting your self-esteem and building your Womanpower is an ongoing process. We all meet many obstacles and circumstances in our lives that we want to overcome with power, grace, and self-esteem.

Return to the quizzes as circumstances in your life change.

Once you have mastered the Womanpower Boosting Cycle, you are set for life. Whether you are a teenager or an older adult, you can use the skills learned from the Boosting Cycle to help you every day. You will be better prepared to deal with the manipulators and aggressors in your life who might try to take advantage of you, put you down, or try to control you. Now you know that you don't have to let them get away with that kind of behavior. With boosted self-esteem, you know that you can take care of yourself.

Every day, remind yourself: *YOU ARE THE MOST IMPORTANT PERSON YOU KNOW*. You deserve to take good care of yourself at all times. You deserve to influence others to treat you accordingly, and if they don't, you know that you have options and alternatives. You don't have to suffer in silence and take abuse from anyone who tries to squash your self-esteem by treating you poorly. Now you know that they can only do it if you allow them to. Remember, *YOU ARE IN CHARGE OF YOUR LIFE*.

Summarizing the Womanpower Boosting Cycle

Awareness gives you an understanding of what you are doing. Think of awareness as taking a picture of yourself. Look at the picture and see what is going on, what you like, what you don't like, where the behavior comes from, how it feels, and what you would like to change.

Acceptance is taking responsibility for what you become aware of; it is the opposite of blaming others for what you do or are. With *awareness* and *acceptance,* you can change your behaviors from automatic, habitual ones to conscious behaviors of your choice.

Alternatives is the step during which you consider your personal boosters rather than your personal squashers. During the Alternatives phase, examine your choices and learn your new options for behavior changes.

Action means taking the energy you have gained from awareness, acceptance, and consideration of alternatives and using it to go forward. Make affirmations or contracts with yourself to encourage and reinforce those behaviors you have chosen to change.

Use Boosters That Work for You

You get power boosters from others. You can also give yourself boosters. Learn to listen to your boosters, not your squashers. When you hear squashers, counteract them with your own personal boosters. Now you know how.

With improved self-esteem, you will feel better about your relationship with yourself, your parents, friends, or lovers, your husband or boss, as well as your own children, if you are a mother. It will enable you to be equal in friendships, marital or sexual relationships, and more equal in relationships at school or work. Improved self-esteem will help you find the power to release yourself from feelings of entrapment if you are now in a codependent relationship.

When new situations come up, look back over your quizzes and determine what power boosters worked for you in the past. You'll rediscover previously used—and unused—boosters ready to help you up from your position of squashed power and self-esteem.

Let Go of Secrets and Old Fears

The energy you use to keep secrets may drain your self-esteem. Consider the benefit/risk ratio of telling or not telling. In many cases, unburdening will not make others think any less of you but may cause them to respect you in new ways when they understand more about you.

In workshops, Sheila holds up a soft, little pillow to dramatize an important point. *Fear detracts from power.* One side of the pillow is labeled FEAR; the other side is labeled POWER. The little pillow is a good metaphor for self-esteem. Sheila demonstrates four simple maneuvers to show how fear can keep you from going forward in life as a powerful self.

Think of yourself holding the two-sided pillow in front of you. You are hiding behind it, with the FEAR side facing forward. When you hide behind your fears, they sap your energy and pull you down. They stop you from getting ahead and feeling your power. You may fear a negative outcome. Doing so hides your own power from you. You stay stuck.

Next, put the pillow behind you. Hide the FEAR sign as well as the POWER sign from other people. When you do that, you are also denying both fear and power to *yourself.* This makes you anxious, because in this process, you are still feeding the fear by hiding it behind you. Your body language and your non-verbal language shows it.

Take the pillow firmly in both hands. Pound it! Pound it again! Think of how you have been "pounding yourself," beating up on yourself because you felt stuck. While pounding yourself, you were also pounding down your self-esteem and power. Now you know how depowering feeling stuck can be. Then take the pillow and toss it across the room. Feel the relief. Now you've thrown away your fears and they can't reach you anymore.

Slowly and deliberately, walk across the room. Bend and gently lift the pillow. Smile at the POWER side. Pat the pillow on its POWER side. Stroke the pillow on both sides. This means that you are acknowledging the fear as a legitimate part of you, not to be denied, demeaned or hidden. As you acknowledge your fear, you are also acknowledging your power. Take care of yourself. Love yourself for what you are. Empower yourself.

Grow Older, Grow Wiser

Women of all ages have concerns about their self-esteem. While young women may worry about clear skin or a developing bosom, the young working mother worries about being "Super Mom." The older woman worries about losing her sense of autonomy when she no longer is able to maintain her checkbook and handle her investments independently. All this is part of the life cycle. The Womanpower Boosting Cycle can work for readers at any age.

At all ages, women are organizing networks for business purposes as well as social support. Women in many professions are developing increasing strength through unity with their peers. Connections help reinforce self-esteem. Women in support groups realize that they are not "different" because they have a particular social problem or health concern. Support groups also help them realize they are not alone. Across the country, hundreds of women's health centers have been organized to provide health education as well as social support for women. Women can be a resource for others. As we empower ourselves, we empower others.

New Opportunities: New Generations, New Worlds

This is the era of opportunities for women. This is the generation with two women as Supreme Court justices and many women in high places throughout government. We have women astronauts. Mothers have greater expectations for their daughters. Middle-aged women have different expectations of themselves.

Women have new identities. A dramatic example is an alumni group of women who graduated college in the mid-1950s. At their first reunion, five years after graduation, each introduced herself with her name and "my husband is . . ." Years later, at their fortieth reunion, sixty women stood up and introduced themselves: "I'm a volunteer with *xxxxx,* I'm president of *xxxx,* I'm director of *xxxx,* I just completed my *XXXXX."* You get the idea. They had identities of their own! These women had found themselves; they were not dependent on anyone else for an identity. A high percentage still had their original husbands, some had second and third husbands, some were widowed or divorced. Many were grandmothers. Only one women of the sixty had not married.

Be Confident: Be at Peace with Yourself

We came across a poem that we would like to share with you. It was brought to our attention by our friend Chin-Ing Helen Chen. It was written in 1991 by Thich Nhat Hanh, a Vietnamese monk. It expresses the freedom you will feel when you have freed yourself of unwanted burdens from the past and moved on with more confidence.

We Are All Flowers*

Breathing in, I know that I am breathing in.
Breathing out, I know I am breathing out.
In/Out.

Breathing in, I see myself as a flower.
Breathing out, I feel fresh.
Flower/Fresh.

Breathing in, I see myself as a mountain.
Breathing out, I feel solid.
Mountain/Solid.

* *Adapted from* Touching Peace: Practicing the Art of Mindful Living *by Thich Nhat Hanh, Parallax Press, Berkeley, California, 1992. Reprinted by permission.*

Breathing in, I see myself as still water.
Breathing out, I reflect things as they are.
Water/Reflecting.

Breathing in, I see myself as space.
Breathing out, I feel free.
Space/Free.

Be Your Own Heroine

You can be your own heroine after working through the four "A"s of the Womanpower Boosting Cycle. You can use the steps every day of your life. Life is not always a smooth road. When you encounter a bump in the road, or a stuck spot, go back to the four "A"s. Determine which step will help you: *Awareness, Acceptance, Alternatives,* or *Action!*

Learn from your own past experiences. Here are a few reminders:

- Keep yourself looking as good as possible. You will feel empowered when you know you look well.

- Consider your positive characteristics. Don't compare yourself to others, assuming they are more attractive, competent, or popular.

- Accept imperfections in yourself as well as others. Everyone drops some of the balls they juggle at times. Keep the important ones in the air.

- Use assertiveness skills to decrease your vulnerability to those who want to demean you.

- Consider the sources of your past or present squashers. Understand them. Use the *Action* step of the Womanpower Boosting Cycle.

Identify ways in which you can get what you want and take more powerful control of your life. Tell yourself, at any age, *"I'm Me, I'm The Most Important Person I Know; I'm Doing the Best I Can; I'm Making the Most of What I Have; I love myself. I'm powerful! I'm my own heroine!"*

READING LIST

Abuse

Bass, Ellen. *Beginning to Heal: A First Book for Survivors of Child Sexual Abuse.* New York: Harper-Collins Publishers, 1993.

Bass, Ellen, and Laura Davis. *The Courage to Heal: A Guide for Women Survivors of Child Sexual Abuse.* New York: Harper & Row, 1988.

Fredrickson, Renee. *Repressed Memories: A Journey to Recovery from Sexual Abuse.* New York: Simon and Schuster, 1992.

Maltz, Wendy. *The Sexual Healing Journey: A Guide for Survivors of Sexual Abuse.* New York: Harper-Collins Publishers, 1991.

Patterson, Richard North. *Eyes of a Child.* New York: Knopf: 1995.

Pendegast, Mark. *Victims of Memory: Incest Accusations and Shattered Lives.* Hinesburg, VT: Upper Access Books. 1995.

Ryan, Michael. *Secret Life: An Autobiography.* New York: Pantheon Books, 1995.

Voight, Cynthia. *When She Hollers.* New York: Scholastic, 1994.

Wakefield, Holliday. *Return of the Furies: An Investigation into Recovered Memory Therapy.* Chicago: Open Court, 1994.

Agoraphobia

Ballenger, Janes C. (ed.) *Biology of Agoraphobia.* Washington, D.C.: American Psychiatric Press, 1984.

Frampton, Muriel. *Agoraphobia: Coping with the World Outside.* Wellingborough, England: Turnstone Press, 1984.

Goldstein, Alan J. *Overcoming Agoraphobia: Conquering Fear of the Outside World.* New York: Viking, 1987.

Mathew, A. M., M. G. Gelder, and D. W. Johnston. *Agoraphobia: Nature and Treatment.* New York: Guilford Press, 1981.

Paolino, Adele. *Agoraphobia: Are Panic and Phobias Psychological or Physical?* Winona, MN: Apollo Books, 1984.

Scrignar, Chester R. *From Panic to Peace of Mind: Overcoming Panic and Agoraphobia.* New Orleans: Brunn Press, 1991.

Alcoholism

Berger, Gilda. *Alcoholism and the Family.* New York: F. Watts, 1993.

Diamond, Arthur. *Alcoholism.* San Diego, CA: Lucent Books, 1992.

Dick, R. *New Light on Alcoholism.* Corte Madera, CA: Good Book Publishing, 1994.

Dorsman, Jerry. *How to Quit Drinking Without AA: A Complete Self-Help Guide,* rev. 2nd ed. Rocklin, CA: Prima Publishers, 1994.

Landau, Elaine. *Teenage Drinking.* Hillside, NJ: Enslow, 1994.

Liehelt, Robert A. *Straight Talk About Alcoholism.* New York: Pharos Books, 1992.

O'Farrell, Timothy J., Carolyn A. Weyand, with Diane Logan. *Alcohol and Sexuality: An Annotated*

Bibliography on Alcohol Use, Alcoholism, and Human Sexual Behavior. Phoenix, AZ: Oryx Press, 1983.

Rosenberg, Maxine B. *Not My Family: Sharing the Truth About Alcoholism.* New York: Bradbury Press, 1988.

Seixas, Judith S., and Geraldine Youcha. *Children of Alcoholism: A Survivor's Manual.* New York: Crown Publishers, 1985.

St. Clair, Harvey R. *Recognizing Alcoholism and Its Effects: A Mini-Guide.* New York: Karger, 1991.

Varley, Chris. *Alcoholism.* New York: M. Cavendish, 1994.

Woititz, Janet Geringer. *Adult Children of Alcoholics.* Deerfield Beach, FL: Health Communications, 1990.

Alternative Therapies

Bensky, Dan, and Andres Gamble. *Chinese Herbal Medicine, Materia Medica.* Seattle, WA: Eastland, 1986.

Feldenkrais, Moshe. *Awareness Through Movement.* New York: Harper & Row, 1977.

Frawley, David. *Ayurvedic Healing: A Comprehensive Guide.* Salt Lake City, UT: Passage Press, 1989.

_____ and Vasant Lad. *The Yoga of Herbs: An Ayurvedic Guide to Herbal Medicine.* Santa Fe., NM: Lotus Press, 1986.

Heyn, Birgit. *Ayurveda: The Indian Art of Natural Medicine & Life Extension.* Rochester, VT: Healing Arts Press, 1990.

Kaminski, Patricia, and Richard Katz. *Flower Essence Repertory. A Comprehensive Guide to North American and English Flower Essences for Emotional and Spiritual Well-Being.* Nevada City, CA: The Flower Essence Society, 1994.

Lad, Dr. Vasant. *Ayurveda: The Science of Self-Healing—A Practical Guide.* Santa Fe, NM: Lotus Press, 1984.

Reid, Daniel. *The Complete Book of Chinese Health and Healing.* Boston: Shambhala, 1994.

Ryman, Danielle. *Aromatherapy. The Complete Guide to Plant and Flower Essences for Health and Beauty.* New York: Bantam Books, 1991.

Anorexia, Bulimia, and Eating Disorders

Abraham, Suzanne. *Eating Disorders: The Facts.* Oxford, England: Oxford University Press, 1984.

Cassell, Dana K. *Encyclopedia of Obesity and Eating Disorders.* New York: Facts on File, 1994.

Heater, Sandra Harvey. *Am I Still Visible? A Woman's Triumph Over Anorexia Nervosa.* White Hall, VA: White Hall Books, 1983.

Kinoy, Barbara P., ed. *Eating Disorders: New Directions in Treatment and Recovery.* New York: Columbia University Press, 1994.

Meltsner, Susan. *Body & Soul: A Guide to Lasting Recovery from Compulsive Eating and Bulimia.* Center City, MN: Hazelden, 1993.

Mitchell, James E., ed. *Anorexia Nervosa and Bulimia: Diagnosis and Treatment.* Minneapolis, MN: University of Minnesota Press, 1985.

Neuman, Patricia A. *Anorexia Nervosa and Bulimia: A Handbook for Counselors and Therapists.* New York: Van Nostrand Reinhold, 1983.

Orbach, Susie. *Hunger Strike: An Anorexic's Struggle as a Metaphor for Our Age.* New York: Norton, 1986.

Romeo, Felicia F. *Understanding Anorexia Nervosa.* Springfield, IL: C. C. Thomas, 1986.

Sacker, Ira M. *Dying to Be Thin.* New York: Warner Books, 1987.

Sonder, Ben. *Eating Disorders: When Food Turns Against You.* New York: F. Watts, 1993.

White, Marlene B. *Bulimarexia: The Binge/Purge Cycle*. New York: Norton, 1983.

Woodman, Marion. *The Owl Was a Baker's Daughter: Obesity, Anorexia Nervosa, and the Repressed Feminine, a Psychological Study*. Toronto: Inner City Books, 1980.

Anxiety and Anxiety Disorders
(*See also* Phobias; Obsessive-Compulsive Disorder; Post-Traumatic Stress Disorder)

Agras, M. W. *Panic: Facing Fears, Phobias, and Anxiety*. New York: W. H. Freeman, 1985.

Barlow, D. H. *Anxiety and Its Disorders: The Nature and Treatment of Anxiety and Panic*. New York: The Guilford Press, 1988.

Barlow, D. H., and J.A. Cerny. *The Psychological Treatment of Panic*. New York: The Guilford Press, 1988.

Beck, Aaron. *Anxieties and Phobias*. New York: Basic Books, 1985.

Bourne, Edmund J. *The Anxiety and Phobia Workbook*. Oakland: New Harbinger, 1990.

Gold, Mark S. *The Good News About Panic, Anxiety & Phobias*. New York: Bantam Books, 1990.

Goodwin, D. W. *Anxiety*. New York: Oxford University Press, 1986.

Gorman, J. M., M. R. Leibowitz, and D. F. Klein. *Panic Disorders and Agoraphobia*. Kalamazoo, MI: Current Concepts in Medicine, 1984.

Marks, Isaac. *Living with Fear*. New York: McGraw-Hill, 1980.

Nardo, Don. *Anxiety and Phobias*. New York: Chelsea House, 1992.

Ornstein, Robert, and David S. Sobel. "Calming Anxiety, Phobias and Panic. *Mental Medicine Update* vol. III, no. 3 (1994).

Ross, Jerilyn. *Triumph Over Fear: A Book of Help and*

Hope for People with Anxiety, Panic Attacks, and Phobias. New York: Bantam Books, 1994.

Sheehan, David. *The Anxiety Disease and How to Overcome It.* New York: Charles Scribner & Sons, 1984.

Taylor, C. Barr, and Bruce Arnow. *The Nature and Treatment of Anxiety Disorders.* New York: Free Press, 1988.

Wolman, Benjamin, and George Sticker. *Anxiety and Related Disorders: A Handbook.* New York: John Wiley and Sons, 1991.

Body Image

Bordo, Susan. *Unbearable Weight; Feminism, Western Culture, and the Body.* Berkeley: University of California Press, 1993.

Chapkis, Wendy. *Beauty Secrets: Women and the Politics of Appearance.* Boston: South End Press, 1986.

Chernin, Kim. *The Obsession: Reflections of the Tyranny of Slenderness.* New York: Harper & Row, 1982.

Garrison, Terry Nicholetti, with David Levitsky. *Fed Up: A Woman's Guide to Freedom from the Diet/Weight Prison.* New York: Carroll & Graf, 1993.

Hall, Lindsey, ed. *Full Lives: Women Who Have Freed Themselves from Food & Weight Obsessions.* Carlsbad, CA: Gurze Books, 1993.

Hillman, Carolynn. *Love Your Looks: How to Stop Criticizing and Start Appreciating Your Appearance.* New York: Fireside Books, Simon and Schuster, 1996.

Hirschmann, Jane R., and Munter, Carol H. *When Women Stop Hating Their Bodies: Freeing Yourself from Food and Weight Obsession.* New York: Fawcett, 1995.

Hirschmann, Jane R., and Carol N. Munter. *Overcoming Overeating.* New York: Fawcett Columbine, 1988.

Hutchinson, Marcia Germaine. *Transforming Body Image.* Trumansburg, NY: Crossing Press, 1985.

Kano, Susan. *Making Peace with Food: Freeing Yourself from the Diet/Weight Obsession.* New York: Harper & Row, 1989.

Naidus, Beverly. *One Size Does Not Fit All.* Littleton, CO: Aigis Publications, 1993.

Newman, Leslea. *Fat Chance.* New York: G. P. Putnam's Sons, 1994.

Roth, Geneen. *Breaking Free from Compulsive Eating.* New York: Plume, 1993.

Seid, Roberta. *Never Too Thin: Why Women Are at War with Their Bodies.* New York: Prentice Hall, 1989.

Wolf, Naomi. *The Beauty Myth.* New York: Doubleday, 1991.

Depression and Manic-Depressive Disorder

Bohn, John, and James W. Jefferson. *Lithium and Manic Depression: A Guide.* Lithium Information Center, University of Wisconsin, Madison, WI (revised, 1990).

Burns, David D. *Feeling Good: The New Mood Therapy.* New York: Morrow, 1980.

DePaulo, J. Raymond, and Keith Ablo. *How to Cope with Depression: A Complete Guide for You and Your Family.* NJ: McGraw Hill, 1989.

Greist, John H., and James W. Jefferson. *Depression and Its Treatment: Help for the Nation's #1 Mental Problem.* Washington, DC: American Psychiatric Press, Inc., 1984.

Papolos, Demitri, and Janic Palolos. *Overcoming Depression.* New York: Harper & Row, 1987.

Winokur, G. *Depression: The Facts*. New York: Oxford University Press, 1981.

Guided Imagery

Achterberg, Jeanne. *Imagery in Healing: Shamanism and Modern Medicine*. San Francisco: Shambhala Publications, 1985.

Burns, David. *Feeling Good: The New Mood Therapy*. New York: Avon Books, 1992.

Epstein, Gerald. *Healing Visualizations, Creating Healing Through Imagery*. New York: Bantam Books, 1989.

Rossman, Martin L. *Healing Yourself: A Step-by-Step Program for Better Health Through Imagery*. New York: Walker, 1987.

Samuels, Michael. *Healing with the Mind's Eye*. New York: Random House, 1992.

Siegel, Bernie. *Love, Medicine and Miracles*. New York: Harper & Row, 1986.

_____. *Peace, Love and Healing*. New York, Harper & Row, 1986.

Simonton, O. Carl, Stephanie Matthews-Simonton, and James L. Creighton. *Getting Well Again*. New York: Bantam Books, 1981.

Headaches

Diamond, Seymour. *The Hormone Headache: New Ways to Prevent, Manage and Treat Migraines and Other Headaches*. NY: Macmillan, 1995

Inlander, Charles B. *47 Ways to Stop the Pain*. New York: Walker and Co., 1995.

Minirth, Frank B. with Sandy Dengler. *The Headache Book*. Nashville, TN: Nelson Publishers, 1994.

Rapoport, Alan M. *Headache Relief: A Comprehensive, Up-to-Date, Medically Proven Program That*

Can Control and Ease Headache Pain. NY: Simon and Schuster, 1990.

Solomon, Seymour, and Steven Fraccaro. *The Headache Book.* Yonkers, NY: Consumer Reports Books, 1991.

Meditation

Benson, Herbert. *The Relaxation Response.* New York: Avon Books, 1975.

_____. *Beyond the Relaxation Response.* New York: Berkeley Press, 1985.

Borysenko, Joan, and Duscher, J. *On Wings of Light: Meditations for Awakening to the Source.* New York: Warner, 1992.

Chopra, Deepak. *Ageless Body, Timeless Mind.* New York: Crown, 1993.

_____. *Unconditional Life.* New York: Bantam, 1992.

_____. *Creating Health.* Boston: Houghton Mifflin, 1991.

_____. *Quantum Healing.* New York: Bantam, 1989.

Connor, Danny, with Michael Tse. *Qigeng. Chinese Movement & Meditation for Health.* York Beach, ME: Samuel Weiser, 1992.

Cousins, Norman. *The Healing Heart.* New York: Norton, 1983.

Dossey, L. *Meaning and Medicine; A Doctor's Tales of Breakthrough and Healing.* New York: Bantam, 1991.

_____. *Recovering the Soul.* New York: Bantam, 1989.

_____. *Space, Time and Medicine.* Boston, Shambhala, 1982.

Dychtwald, K. *Bodymind.* Los Angeles: Tarcher, 1986.

Goleman, Daniel. *The Meditative Mind.* Los Angeles: Tarcher, 1988.

Hanh, Thich Nhat. *Being Peace*. Berkeley: Parallax Press, 1987.

Kabat-Zinn, Jon. *Wherever You Go, There You Are*, New York, Hyperion, 1994.

_____. *Full Catastrophe Living: Using the Wisdom of Your Body and Mind to Face Stress, Pain and Illness*. New York: Delacorte Press, 1991.

Levey, Daniel. *The Fine Arts of Relaxation, Concentration and Meditation*. London: Wisdom Publications, 1987.

Nuernberger, Phil. *Freedom from Stress*. Honesdale, PA: The Himalayan International Institute of Yoga Science and Philosophy, 1985.

Trungpa, Chogyam. *Shambhala: The Sacred Path of the Warrior*. Boston: Shambhala, 1984.

Mind/Body Healing

Borysenko, Joan. *Guilt Is the Teacher, Love Is the Lesson*. New York: Warner, 1991.

_____. *Minding the Body, Mending the Mind*. New York: Bantam, 1988.

Cannon, Walter. *The Wisdom of the Body*. New York: Norton, 1939.

Cousins, Norman. *Head First: The Biology of Hope and the Healing Power of the Human Spirit*. New York: Viking Penguin, 1990.

_____. *The Healing Heart*. New York: Norton, 1983.

_____. *Anatomy of an Illness as Perceived by the Patient*. New York: Norton, 1979.

Dienstfrey, Harris. *Where the Mind Meets the Body*. New York: HarperCollins, 1991.

Dossey, Larry. *Space, Time and Medicine*. Boston: Shambhala, 1982.

Goleman, Daniel, and Joel Gurin, eds. *Mind Body Medicine: How to Use Your Mind for Better Health*. Yonkers, N.Y: Consumer Reports Books, 1993.

Gordon, James S., et al. *Mind, Body and Health: Toward an Integral Medicine.* New York: Human Sciences Press, 1984.

Locke, Steven E., and Douglas Colligan. *The Healer Within: The New Medicine of Mind and Body.* New York: NAL-Dutton, 1987.

Moyers, B. *Healing and the Mind.* New York: Doubleday, 1993.

Ornstein, Robert, and David Sobel. *The Healing Brain.* New York: Simon and Schuster, 1988.

Pelletier, Kenneth R. *Mind as Healer, Mind as Slayer,* rev. ed. New York: Delacorte, 1992.

_____. *Holistic Medicine: From Stress to Optimum Health.* Magnolia, Mass.: Peter Smith, 1984.

Siegel, Bernie. *Peace, Love and Healing.* New York: Harper and Row, 1989.

_____. *Love, Medicine and Miracles.* New York: Harper and Row, 1986.

Williams, Redford. *The Trusting Heart: Great News About Type A Behavior.* New York: Times Books, 1989.

Nutrition

Brody, Jane. *Jane Brody's Nutrition Book.* New York: W. W. Norton, 1981.

Brown, Judith E. *Everywoman's Guide to Nutrition.* Minneapolis: University of Minnesota Press, 1991.

Finn, Susan Calvert, and Linda Stern Kass. *The Real Life Nutrition Book: Making the Right Food Choices Without Changing Your Life-Style.* New York: Penguin Books, 1992.

Haas, Robert. *Eat Smart, Think Smart: How to Use Nutrients and Supplements to Achieve Maximum Mental and Physical Performance.* New York: HarperCollins, 1994.

Kotsanis, Frank N., and Maureen A. Mackey, eds. *Nutrition in the '90s: Current Controversies and Analysis. Vol 2.* New York: M. Dekker, 1994.

Lark, Susan M. *The Women's Health Companion: Self-Help Nutrition Guide & Cookbook*. Berkeley: Celestial Arts, 1994.

Manahan, William O. *Eat for Health: A Do-It-Yourself Nutrition Guide for Solving Common Medical Problems*. Tiburon, CA: H. J. Kramer, 1988.

Quillan, Patrick. *Beating Cancer with Nutrition*. Tulsa, OK: Nutrition Times Press, 1994.

Tessler, Gordon, S. *Lazy Person's Guide to Better Nutrition*. La Jolla, CA: Better Health Publishers, 1984.

Werbach, Melvyn. *Healing Through Nutrition: A Natural Approach to Treating 50 Common Illnesses with Diet and Nutrients*. New York: HarperCollins, 1993.

Obsessive-Compulsive Disorder

Alper, Gerald. *The Puppeteers: Studies of Obsessive Control*. New York: Fromm International Publishing Corporation, 1994.

Reyes, Karen. "Obsessive-Compulsive Disorder: There Is Help," *Modern Maturity* (November–December 1995).

Phobias
(See also Anxiety Disorders)

Doctor, Ronald M., and Ada P. Kahn. *Encyclopedia of Phobias, Fears and Anxieties*. New York: Facts on File, 1989.

DuPont, Robert L. *Phobia: A Comprehensive Summary of Modern Treatments*. New York: Brunner/Mazel, 1982.

Jampolsky, Gerald. *Love Is Letting Go of Fear*. New York: Bantam Books, 1979.

Marks, Isaac M. *Fears, Phobias, and Rituals*. Oxford England: Oxford University Press, 1987.

_____. *Living with Fear.* New York: McGraw-Hill, 1980.

Marshall, John R. *Social Phobia: From Shyness to Stage Fright.* New York: Basic Books, 1994.

Zane, Manuel D., and Harry Milt. *Your Phobia.* Washington, DC: American Psychiatric Press, Inc., 1984.

Post-Traumatic Stress Disorder

Egendorf, A. *Healing from the War: Trauma and Transformation After Vietnam.* New York: Houghton Mifflin, 1985.

Eitinger, Leo, and Robert Krell, with Miriam Rieck. *The Psychological and Medical Effects of Concentration Camps and Related Persecutions on Survivors of the Holocaust.* Vancouver: University of British Columbia Press, 1985.

Eth, S., and R. S. Pynoos. *Post-Traumatic Stress Disorder in Children.* Washington, DC: American Psychiatric Press, Inc., 1985.

Lindy, Jacob D. *Vietnam: A Casebook.* New York: Brunner/Mazel, 1987.

Peterson, Kirtland C., Maurice F. Prout, and Robert A. Schwarz. *Post-Traumatic Stress Disorder: A Clinician's Guide.* New York: Plenum Press, 1991.

Sonnenberg, S. M., A. S. Blank, and J. A. Talbott, eds. *The Trauma of War: Stress and Recovery in Vietnam Veterans.* Washington, DC: American Psychiatric Press, 1985.

Van der Kolk, B. A., ed. *Post-Traumatic Stress Disorder: Psychological and Biological Sequelae.* Washington, DC: American Psychiatric Press, Inc.

Psychology and Self-Esteem

Berne, Eric. *Games People Play.* New York: Grove Press, 1964.

Borysenko, Joan. *Guilt Is The Teacher, Love Is the Lesson.* New York: Warner Books, 1990.

Bradshaw, John. *Bradshaw On: The Family.* Deerfield Beach, FL: Health Communications, Inc., 1988.

_____. *Healing the Shame That Binds You.* Deerfield Beach, FL: Health Communications, Inc., 1988.

Cousins, Norman. *The Healing Heart.* New York: Avon Books, 1984.

Csikzentmihalyi, Mihaly. *Flow: The Psychology of Optimal Experience.* New York: Harper Collins Perennial, 1991.

Peck, M. Scott. *The Road Less Traveled.* New York: Simon and Schuster, 1978.

Wolinsky, Stephen H. *Trances People Live: Healing Approaches in Quantum Psychology.* Norfolk, CT: Bramble Co., 1991.

Relaxation

Agras, W. S., C. B. Taylor, H. C. Kraemer, M. A. Southam, and J. A. Schneider. "Relaxation Training for Essential Hypertension at the Worksite: II. The Poorly Controlled Hypertensive," *Psychosomatic Medicine 49* (1987): 264–273.

Benson, Herbert. *Your Maximum Mind.* New York: Times Books, 1987.

_____. *Beyond the Relaxation Response.* New York: Berkeley Press, 1985.

_____. *The Relaxation Response.* New York: Avon Books, 1975.

_____, Eileen M. Stuart, and staff of the Mind/Body Medical Institute. *The Wellness Book: The Comprehensive Guide to Maintaining Health and Treating Stress-Related Illness.* New York: Carol, 1992.

Blumenfeld, Larry, ed. *The Big Book of Relaxation:*

Simple Techniques to Control the Excess Stress in Your Life. Roslyn, NY: Relaxation Company, 1994.

Davis, Martha, Elizabeth Robbins Eshelman, and Matthew McKay. *The Relaxation and Stress Reduction Workbook.* Oakland: New Harbinger Publications, 1995.

Self-Esteem

Bower, Bruce. "Gender Paths Wind Toward Self-Esteem." *Science News* 143 (May 15, 1993): 308.

Branden, Nathaniel. *How to Raise Your Self-Esteem.* New York: Bantam Books, 1988.

Douglas, Susan J. *Where the Girls Are: Growing Up Female with the Mass Media.* New York: Random House, 1994.

Dritchell, Theda. "How Healthy Is Your Self-Esteem?" *Cosmopolitan* 215 (August 1993): 136.

Faludi, Susan. *Backlash: The Undeclared War Against American Women.* New York: Anchor/Doubleday, 1991.

Friedan, Betty. *The Fountain of Age.* New York: Simon and Schuster, 1993.

Friedman, Howard S. *The Self-Healing Personality.* New York: Penguin Books, 1992.

Hazelton, Deborah M. *Solving the Self-Esteem Puzzle.* Deerfield Beach, FL: Health Communications, Inc., 1991.

Jones, Riki Robbins. *The Empowered Woman.* New York: Shapolsky Publishers, 1992.

Maynard, Rona. "Boosting Self-Esteem," *Chatelaine* 64 (March 1991): 188.

McKay, Matthew, and Patrick Fanning. *Self-Esteem.* Oakland: New Harbinger Publications, 1987.

Moeller, Thomas G. "What Research Says about Self-Esteem and Academic Performance," *Education Digest* 59 (January 1994): 34.

Semigran, Candace. *One-Minute Self-Esteem: Caring for Yourself and Others.* New York: Bantam Books, 1990.

Social Support and Self-Help

Brothers, Joyce. *Positive Plus: The Practical Plan for Liking Yourself Better.* New York: G. P. Putnam's Sons, 1994.

Flores, Bettina. *Chiquitas's Cocoon: A Self-help Guide for the Latina Woman.* New York: Villard Books, 1994.

Pilisuk, Marc, and Susan H. Parks. *The Healing Web: Social Networks and Human Survival.* Hanover, NH: University Press of New England, 1986.

Spiegel, David. *Living Beyond Limits.* New York: Times Books, 1993.

Ullman, Jeffrey. *12 Secrets for Finding Love and Commitment.* New York: Simon and Schuster, 1995.

White, Barbara J., and Edward J. Madara. *The Self-Help Sourcebook: Finding & Forming Mutual Aid Self-Help Groups.* Denville, NJ: American Self-Help Clearinghouse, St. Clares-Riverside Medical Center, 1992.

White, Thayer. *Be Your Own Therapist: Whoever You Hire Is Just Your Assistant.* San Francisco: Purple Paradox Press, 1995.

Wilson, Paul. *Instant Calm: Over 100 Easy-to-Use Techniques for Relaxing Mind and Body.* New York: Plume, 1995.

Stress and Stress Management for Better Self-Esteem

Brammer, L. M. *How to Cope with Life Transitions: The Challenge of Personal Change.* New York: Hemisphere Publishing, 1991.

Eliot, Robert S. *From Stress to Strength: How to Lighten Your Load and Save Your Life.* New York: Bantam Books, 1994.

Feder, Barnaby J. "A Spreading Pain, and Cries for Justice." *The New York Times* (June 5, 1994).

Faelten, Sharon, and David Diamond. *Take Control of Your Life: A Complete Guide to Stress Relief.* Emmaus, PA: Rodale Press, 1988.

Gordon, James S. *Stress Management.* New York: Chelsea House Publishers, 1990.

Lark, Susan M. *Anxiety and Stress: A Self-Help Program.* Los Altos, CA. Westchester Publishing Company, 1993.

Miller, Lyle H. and Alma Dell Smith. *The Stress Solution: An Action Plan to Manage the Stress in Your Life.* New York: Pocket Books, Division of Simon and Schuster, 1993.

Ornish, Dean. *Stress, Diet, and Your Heart.* New York: Holt, Rinehart and Winston, 1983.

Patel, Chandra. *The Complete Guide to Stress Management.* New York: Plenum Press, 1991.

Gillespie, Peggy Roggenbuck. *Less Stress in 30 Days.* New York: New American Library, 1986.

Sapolsky, Robert M. *Why Zebras Don't Get Ulcers.* New York: W. H. Freeman & Company, 1994.

Selye, Hans. *The Stress of Life,* rev. ed. New York: McGraw Hill Book Company, 1978.

_____. *Stress Without Distress.* New York: Lipincott, 1974.

Seaward, Brian Luke. *Managing Stress: Principles and Strategies for Health and Wellbeing; Managing Stress: A Creative Journal.* Boston: Jones and Bartless Publishers, 1994.

Snyder, Solomon H., ed. *Stress Management.* New York: Chelsea House Publishers, 1990.

Women/Gender Roles

Belenky, Mary Field, Blythe McVicker Clinchy, Nancy Rule Goldberger, and Jill Mattuck Tarule.

Women's Ways of Knowing. New York: Basic Books, 1986.

Berg, Barbara J. *The Crisis of the Working Mother.* New York: Summit Books, 1986.

Freudenberger, Herbert, and Gail North. *Women's Burnout: How to Spot It, How to Reverse It, and How to Prevent It.* Garden City, NY: Doubleday & Company, Inc., 1985.

Kahn, Ada P. "Women and Stress." *Sacramento Medicine* (September, 1995).

Lerner, Harriet Goldhor. *The Dance of Intimacy.* New York: Harper & Row, 1989.

_____. *The Dance of Anger.* New York: Harper & Row, 1985.

Long, B. C., and C. J. Haney. "Coping Strategies for Working Women: Aerobic Exercise and Relaxation Interventions. *Behavior Therapy 19* (1988): 75–83.

Powell, J. Robin. *The Working Woman's Guide to Managing Stress.* Englewood Cliffs, NJ: Prentice Hall, 1994.

Witkin-Lanoil, Georgia. *The Female Stress Syndrome: How to Become Stress-Wise in the '90s.* New York, Berkeley Books, 1991.

Workplace and Career

Briles, Judith. *Gender Traps: Conquiring Confrontophobia, Toxic Bosses & Other Landmines at Work.* New York: McGraw Hill, 1996.

Campbell, Sue. "The Girl Revolution" *Glamour* 92 (April 1994). v92 n4 p112(2).

Donkin, Scott W. *Sitting on the Job: How to Survive the Stresses of Sitting Down to Work: A Practical Handbook.* Boston: Houghton Mifflin Company, 1986.

Dumas, Lynne S. "Rejection Is the Single Worst Thing in the World." *Cosmopolitan.* n5 p. 220(4) 213 (November 1992).

Frankenhaeuser, Marianne. "The Psychophysiology of Workload, Stress, and Health: Comparison Between the Sexes." *Annals of Behavioral Medicine* 13(4): 197-204.

Karasek, Robert, and Tores Theorell. *Health Work: Stress, Productivity, and the Reconstruction of Working Life.* New York: Basic Books, 1990.

Paulsen, Barbara. "Work and Play: A Nation Out of Balance." *Health* (October 1994). v8 n6 p44(5).

Repetti, Rena, Karen Matthews, and Ingrid Waldron. "Employment and Women's Health Effect of Paid Employment on Women's Mental and Physical Health." *American Psychologist* 44(11):1394–1401.

Roiphe, Anne. "Raising Daughters (Improving Girls' Self-esteem)." *Working Woman* 19 (April 1994): 42.

Rosen, Robert. *The Healthy Company.* Los Angeles: Jeremy P. Tarcher, 1991.

Schor, Juliet. *The Overworked American: The Unexpected Decline of Leisure.* New York: Basic Books, 1991.

Shalowitz, Deborah. "Another Health-Care Headache: Job Stress Could Strain Corporate Budgets." *Business Insurance* 25 (May 20, 1991).

Somerville, Janice. "Stress Treatment Costing Billions." *American Medical News* (November 10, 1989). v.32 n32 p17(1).

Veninga, Robert L., and James P. Spradley. *The Work/Stress Connection.* Boston: Little, Brown 1981.

Walker, Cathy. "Workplace Stress." *Canadian Dimension* 27 (August 1993). v.27 n4 p29(4).

White, Kate. *Why Good Girls Don't Get Ahead, But Gutsy Girls Do.* New York: Warner Books, 1995.

Alternative Medicine

Baker, Sarah. *The Alexander Technique: The Revolutionary Way to Use Your Body for Total Energy.* New York: Bantam Books, 1978.

Bloomfield, Frena. *Chinese Beliefs.* London: Arrow Books, 1983.

Eisenberg, D., et al. "Unconventional Medicine in the United States: Prevalence, Costs, and Patterns of Use." *New England Journal of Medicine* 328 (1993): 246–252.

Krieger, D. *Therapeutic Touch: How to Use Your Hands to Help or to Heal.* Englewood Cliffs, NJ: Prentice Hall, 1979.

Turner, Roger Newman. *Naturopathic Medicine: Treating the Whole Person.* Northamptonshire, England: Thorsons Publishers, Ltd., 1984.

Biofeedback

Brown, Barbara. *Stress and the Art of Biofeedback.* New York: Harper & Row, 1977.

Karlins, Marvin, and Lewis M. Andrews. *Biofeedback: Turning on the Powers of Your Mind.* New York: J. B. Lippincott, 1972.

Olton, D. S., and A. R. Noonberg. *Biofeedback: Clinical Applications in Behavioral Medicine.* Englewood Cliffs, NJ: Prentice-Hall, 1980.

Eating Disorders

Sands, Melissa. *Chatelaine* 64 (July 1991): 49.

Fertility/Infertility

Liebmann-Smith, Joan. *In Pursuit of Pregnancy: How Couples Discover, Cope With, and Resolve Their Fertility Problems.* New York: Newmarket Press, 1987.

Domar, A. D., M. M. Seibel, and H. Benson. "The Mind/Body Program for Infertility: A New Behavioral Treatment Approach for Women with

Infertility." *Fertility and Sterility* 53 (1990): 246–249.

Mahlstedt. P. "The Psychological Component of Infertility." *Fertility and Sterility* 43 (1985): 335–346.

Seibel, M.M. (ed.) *Infertility: A Comprehensive Test.* Norwalk, Conn.: Appleton & Lange, 1990.

Hypnosis

Erickson, M. H., and E. L. Rossi. *Hypnotherapy: An Exploratory Casebook.* New York: Irvington, 1979.

Rhue J. W., S. J. Lynn, and I. Kirsch, eds. *Handbook of Clinical Hypnosis.* Washington, DC: American Psychological Association, 1993.

Rossi, E. L. *The Psychology of Mind-Body Healing: New Concepts of Therapeutic Hypnosis.* New York: Norton, 1993.

Mindfulness Meditation (Insight Meditation)

Goldstein, Joseph, and Jack Kornfield. *Seeking the Heart of Wisdom: The Path of Insight Meditation.* Boston: Shambhala, 1987.

———. *The Sun My Heart.* Berkeley: Parallax Press, 1988.

———. *The Miracle of Mindfulness: A Manual of Meditation.* Boston: Beacon Press, 1976.

Levine, Stephen. *A Gradual Awakening.* Garden City, NY: Anchor/Doubleday, 1979.

Suzuki, Shunryu. *Zen Mind, Beginner's Mind.* New York: Weatherhill, 1986.

Antonovsky, A. *Unraveling the Mystery of Health: How People Manage Stress and Stay Well.* San Francisco: Jossey-Bass, 1987.

Bridges, W. *Managing Transitions: Making the Most of Change.* Reading, MA: Wesley, 1991.

Bridges, W. Transitions: Making Sense of Life's Changes. Reading, MA: Wesley, 1980.

Colin, Stacey. "How to Find Your Stress Hot Spots." *McCall's* (September 1994). v121 n12 p38(2).

Eliot, Robert, and Dennis Breo. *Is It Worth Dying For?* New York: Bantam Books, 1987.

Maddi, Salvatore, and Suzanne Kobasa. *The Hardy Executive: Health Under Stress.* Homewood, IL: Dow Jones-Irwin, 1984.

Margolis, C. and L. Shrier. *Manual of Stress Management.* Philadelphia: The Franklin Institute Press, 1982.

Wellness and Stress

Barsky, Arthur J. *Worried Sick: Our Troubled Quest for Wellness.* New York: Little, Brown, 1988.

Benson, Herbert. *The Wellness Book: The Complete Guide to Maintaining Health and Treating Stress-Related Illness.* Secaucus, NJ: Carol Publishing Group, 1992.

Bohm, David. *Wholeness and the Implicate Order.* London: Ark., 1980.

Campbell, Joseph. *The Inner Reaches of Outer Space.* New York: Alfred Van Der Marck, 1985.

Capra, Fritjof. *The Turning Point.* New York: Bantam, 1982.

Castenada, Carlos. *The Art of Dreaming.* New York: Harper Collins, 1993.

Dubos, Rene. *Mirage of Health.* New York: Anchor Books, 1959.

Hoffer, Eric. *The True Believer.* New York: Harper and Row, 1951.

Ornstein, Robert, and David Sobel. *The Healing Brain: Breakthrough Discoveries About How the Brain Keeps Us Healthy.* New York: Simon and Schuster, 1987.

Pelletier, Kenneth R. *Sound Mind, Sound Body: A Model for Lifelong Health.* New York: Simon and Schuster, 1994.

Peterson, Christopher, and Lisa M. Bossio. *Health and Optimism.* New York: Macmillan, 1991.

Simonton, Carl. *Getting Well Again.* New York: Bantam Books, 1978.

Strasburg, Kate, et al. *The Quest for Wholeness: An Annotated Bibliography in Patient-Centered Medicine.* Bolinas, CA: Commonweal, 1991.

Stutz, David, and Bernard Feder. *The Savvy Patient: How to Be an Active Participant in Your Medical Care.* Yonkers, NY: Consumer Reports Books, 1990.

Williams, R.W., and V. Williams. *Anger Kills: 17 Strategies for Controlling the Hostility That Can Harm Your Health.* New York: Times Books, 1993.

Wolinsky, Stephen. *Quantum Consciousness: The Guide to Experiencing Quantum Psychology.* Norfolk, CT: Bramble Books, 1993.

Yoga for Wellness and Self-Esteem

Devananda, Swami Vishnu. *The Swivananda Companion to Yoga.* New York: Fireside/Simon and Schuster, 1983.

Groves, Dawn. *Yoga for Busy People: Increase Energy and Reduce Stress in Minutes a Day.* Emeryville, CA: New World Library, 1995.

Iyengar, Geeta S. *Yoga: A Gem for Women.* Palo Alto, CA: Timeless Books, 1990.

Lad, Vasant, and David Frawley. *The Yoga of Herbs,* Santa Fe, NM: Lotus Press, 1986.

Taylor, Louise. *A Woman's Book of Yoga: A Journal for Health and Self-Discovery.* Boston: Charles F. Tuttle Company, 1993.

Terkel, Susan Neiburg. *Yoga Is for Me.* Minneapolis: Lerner Publications Company, 1987.

Vishnudevananda, Swami. *The Complete Illustrated Book of Yoga*. New York: Crown Publishers, Inc., Julian Press, Inc., 1960.

Ada P. Kahn, M.P.H., Ph.D. candidate, is co-author of *Midlife Health: A Woman's Practical Guide to Feeling Good, The A–Z of Women's Sexuality, The Encyclopedia of Mental Health,* and *The Encyclopedia of Phobias, Fears, and Anxieties.*

Kahn is the author of the "Help Yourself to Health" series: *Arthritis, Diabetes, Headaches,* and *High Blood Pressure* and *Diabetes Control and the Kosher Diet.* Her articles have appeared in *Wellness, Psychiatric News, Psychiatric Times, Chicago Medicine, Laboratory Medicine,* and other professional journals.

She has been on the teaching faculties of Columbia College, Chicago, and the University of Health Sciences/The Chicago Medical School, North Chicago, Illinois.

Kahn is Fellow of the American Medical Writers Association (AMWA) and has taught courses in writing and public relations at more than 21 national and regional AMWA meetings. She is a member of The Authors Guild and the American Society of Journalists and Authors.

She received her Master of Public Health (M.P.H.) degree from the School of Medicine, Northwestern University, and Bachelor of Science in Journalism (B.S.J.) degree from Northwestern University. She is a member of the Rotary Club of Evanston.

Since 1990, Kahn has been manager of the Women's Health Program at Rush North Shore Medical Center, Skokie, Illinois. She lives in Evanston, Illinois.

Sheila Kimmel, M.A., is a Chicago-based licensed professional counselor, public speaker, author, trainer, therapist and business consultant with more than 25 years of experience. Her many clients include companies ranging in size from small entrepreneurial corporations to some of the nation's foremost Fortune 500 corporations, associations, community groups, colleges and universities, educators and healthcare professionals.

Kimmel is a certified member of the National Speakers' Association. She motivates her audiences and clients to take the necessary risks to make positive life changes. She has appeared on many television and radio shows speaking on themes of personal growth and personal power. She is the author of *Get Out of Your Own Way,* a self-help book and audiotape. She has also produced audiotapes on topics including "Creative Ways of Managing Stress and Conflict," "Asserting Yourself: Personal Power," and "You Are the Most Important Person You Know."

She holds a Master's degree in counseling psychology from the University of Illinois and has done extensive postgraduate study. She is a member of the Association for Humanistic Psychology and a member of the affiliate staff of Rush North Shore Medical Center, Skokie, Illinois. She lives in Glenview, Illinois.